CHRISTMAS PARTIES

What Do I Do?®

Complete Holiday Fun For:
School
Home
Work
Church
Clubs
Preschool
Youth Groups
Special Events
Ho-Ho-Ho

Award-Winning Author
Wilhelminia Ripple
Illustrated By Heather Anderson

Christmas Parties ... What Do I Do?® Author Wilhelminia Ripple

Oakbrook Publishing House
P.O. Box 2463
Littleton, Colorado 80161-2463
PHONE: (303) 738-1733 • FAX: (303) 797-1995
OR E-MAIL US AT: Oakbrook@whatdoidobooks.com
WEBSITE: http://www.whatdoidobooks.com

To order: 1-888-738-1733

Publisher's Cataloging-in-Publication
(Provided by Quality Books, Inc.)

Ripple, Wilhelminia.
    Christmas parties : what do I do? / author,
Wilhelminia Ripple; illustrator, Heather Anderson;
editor, Dianne Lorang. —1st ed.
    p. cm. — (What do I do)
    Includes index.
    LCCN: 00-132911
    ISBN: 0-9649939-4-5

    1. Christmas. 2. Entertaining — Planning.
3. Holidays—Planning. 4. Christmas decorations.
I. Anderson, Heather. II. Lorang, Dianne. III. Title.

GT4986.AIR57 2000   793.2'2
                        QBI00-500028

Printed and bound in the United States of America.

Printing 10 9 8 7 6 5 4 3 2 1

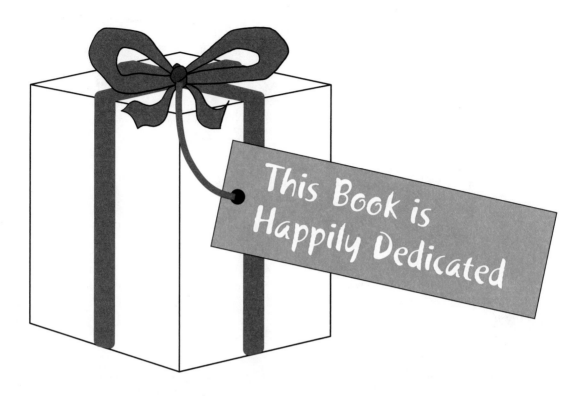

This Book is
Happily Dedicated

To my husband Mark
(who encouraged me when I needed it)
and
To my children Mark, Nick, and Michelle
(for their tolerance and understanding)
and
To all the parents, educators, librarians, retail stores, family, and friends
who asked me to write this book
and
To all who believed in me!

Acknowledgments

Thanks to the children and parents who allowed me to interview them: Maria E. Scordo Allen, Melonie R. Ayers, Sean Ayers, Theresa Ayers, Wally Bronner, Vickie Christiansen, Danielle Dell, Hayley Dell, Richard L. Dmytryshyn, Maria Eusebio, Roger Farrow, Shelley Graham, Mark Hedrick, Jeff Hill, Emily Howard, Holly Kennedy, Pamela Kennedy, Jack Kipnes, Marianne Kipnes, Robin Kuoppala, Henrietta Matteucci, Masako Matumoto, Susan Mead, Dorothy Molstad, Hazel O'Meara, Alice Miller, Mary Muszak, Sharon Reynolds, Margie Ripple, Shalaine Root, Rom Savage, Rudy Savage, Barb Scott, Russell Steven, Katie Stevens, MaryAnn Stevens, Paige Stevens, Jan Tharaldson, Klaus Thiele, Mimi Thiele, Sonya Vo, Sheila Yeatts, and Renee Zumpano

Jolly Thanks to the following for their Santa letters:
Annika Cardoza, Bianca Cardoza, Mark Ripple, Michelle Ripple, and Nick Ripple

Thanks to those who shared a recipe, craft, game, or goody idea with me:
Dolores Arcuri, Shelia Arcuri, Anne Booy, Vera Fosbinder, Barb Johnson, Masako Matumoto, Nancy Rhodes, Sandra Shive, and Renee Zumpano

A Kind Thank You to other authors who shared their sentiment:
Cyndi Duncan and Georgie Patrick - *Nothin' but Muffins, Cookie Exchange,* and *Quick Hors d' oeuvres*
Mary Edsey - *The Best Christmas Decorations in Chicagoland*
Nancy Savage - *Nickel The Baby Bufffalo Who Thought He Was A Dog*
Tom Hegg - *A Cup of Christmas Tea* and *A Memory of Christmas Tea*

A BIG Thank You to the following stores who shared their views:
BRONNER'S CHRISTmas WONDERLAND - Frankenmuth, Michigan
Christmas Manor - Bryan, Ohio
Christmas on the Beach - Toronto, Canada
Forever Christmas - Morro Bay, California
Holiday Displays - Westmont, Illinois
Holiday Haus of Woodstock - Woodstock, Illinois
Samoa Christmas Wreath Gift Shop - Samoa, California
The Christmas Barn - Wilminington, Vermont
The Christmas Mouse - Williamsburg, Norge, and Virginia Beach, Virginia; North Myrtle Beach and Myrtle Beach, South Carolina; Nags Head, North Carolina
Wind River Silks - Anchorage, Alaska
World of Christmas - Park Rapids, Pequot Lakes, Detroit Lakes, and Walker, Minnesota

Thank You to all my friends in the Christmas clubs I was a part of. I'll always remember the laughs, fun, and excitement. Thanks for your opinions, suggestions, and ideas.

Special Thanks to the following who were wonderful to work with:
Cover Design - Bobbi Shupe of E.P. Puffin & Company
Editor - Dianne Lorang of The Write Help
Illustrator - Heather Anderson
Graphic Designer - Rebecca Finkel of F+P Graphic Design, Inc.
Production Assistants - Debbie Foster, Pam Kortman, Liz Lorang, Mark, Michelle, and Nick Ripple

And if I have forgotten you, "Thank You!"

About the Author

Wilhelminia "Willie" Ripple is the award-winning author of the **What Do I Do?**® series. She has twelve years of experience in organizing and creating party ideas. Willie currently lives in Colorado with her husband Mark and their three children.

To learn more about the **What Do I Do?**® series, visit our web site at:
www.whatdoidobooks.com

Table of Contents

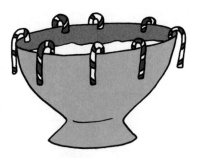

Letters to Santa

Dear Santa,
    I want a barbie
stage and lots of barbies
and some puppets and
Thanks Santa!
And how many elfs
do you have?
            Love,
            DIANA

Dear Santa Clause,
    I want to say that I
want some barbie dollies
and some barbie puppets
and a stage for barbie
puppets Dont forget
the barbie jammies!
And a beutiful red dress.
And how does Comet
fly up in the sky?
            Love,
            AVR KD
And Annika loves Santa!

Dear, Santa
    I know how hard you work,
so I think you should tack a day
off.
    What I want for christmas
is a gotart or seaga chanale
            Nick Ripple

For Christmas
I want kirsten
Or Felicity,
I want the
Dodie Bear
I want
a T.V.
and some
Serprices.
(Surprises)
    Michelle

Dear Santa,
    How, have you been? I've been
a good kid most of the year. What
I want for Christmas is an electric
gautar, some toys, and board games.
Merry Christmas Santa.

            from,
            Mark S. Ripple, Jr.

8

Introduction
How To Use This Book

Christmas Parties…What Do I Do?® gives you the right ideas and hints to help you plan successful and memorable holiday parties for all ages. We at Oakbrook Publishing House know there are other holidays celebrated in the month of December, and do not want to make anyone feel left out. So although we have included a few games, crafts, and goodies for those other holidays (for example, Star of David on page 115), we have focused on Christmas, which is an important holiday not only in the United States but around the world.

The ideas in *Christmas Parties…What Do I Do?*® can be adapted to Christmas parties in schools, for youth groups, at church, at the office, and in your home. This book answers concerns about planning and organizing Christmas parties and contains seven "How-To" chapters—The What, Why, and How of Christmas Parties; Games; Crafts and Favors; Holiday Goodies; Drinks; Christmas Potpourri; and New Year's Tips, and Fun Party Ideas—all designed to help you plan your party with ease.

In the chapters are six themes: Christmas Trees, Stockings, and Candy Canes; Snow, Snowmen, and Snowflakes; Rudolph and His Reindeer; Santa and His Elves, I Believe in Angels; and Christmas Here, There, and Everywhere—Global Celebrations. Go through each chapter and pick the theme that would work best for your party. Feel free to combine different ones, as some of the best parties can come from this added dash of fun.

Everyone loves to be entertained, receive gifts, and be fed, especially at Christmastime, and you will find plenty of ideas in this book to fill those expectations. You can choose from the wide variety of games, crafts, and goodies for adults as well as for children. Each item includes its own list of supplies, step-by-step directions, an illustration, and even pattern pieces when needed.

Be sure to check out the Christmas Potpourri chapter with extra surprises for your guests, and the New Year's Tips, and Fun Party Ideas chapter, full of party ideas, Traditions and Superstitions, and "Midnight Madness" to help you finish off your holiday season the perfect way, having a good time with friends and family.

But first, go to The What, Why, and How of Christmas Parties chapter to learn survival tactics on planning and giving holiday parties. Then, choose a theme—it's the start of any successful party. And don't forget to read the Helpful Hints in the Games, Crafts and Favors, Holiday Goodies, and Drinks chapters, sure to save you unnecessary pitfalls. Remember, *"No more fussing, no more headaches. It couldn't be easier."*

Key To Symbols Used Throughout This Book

Knowledge Symbol
Educational facts relating to the themes, to share with everyone.

Favorite Symbol
Don't miss this game (craft, goody, drink, etc.).

Messy Symbol
Sure to cause dirty hands or faces: Have paper towels ready.

Supply Symbol
Complete list of items needed for each game, craft, goody, drink, etc.

Present Symbol
Easy-to-copy list of all ingredients and supplies needed for each section.

Family Favorite Symbol
Means great family fun!

Note: Throughout the book, we will refer to both genders as "he" for the sake of consistency. "He" can be either female or male.

CHAPTER 1

The What, Why, and How of Christmas Parties

What is a Christmas Party?

A Christmas Party is a get-together to celebrate a very special holiday. It can be as simple as having a few friends or neighbors over for a short visit, or even to bake Christmas cookies or play some games. Christmas Parties can also include club members with groups of over 100 people. There may be office parties to make merry with co-workers. And of course there are family Christmas Parties, traditionally taking place on Christmas Eve or Day. But the one thing they have in common is that each and every party requires planning. In *Christmas Parties...What Do I Do?*® we will focus on how to plan, have, and survive the Christmas Party you've always dreamed about giving.

A Christmas Party can be for adults or children, or can include all ages. It can be as short as an hour or up to several hours long. Guests always enjoy festive food and drinks, as they add to the holiday spirit and season. Be sure to include games and activities to assure plenty of laughter, excitement, and lasting memories.

You could have a rotating dinner, where you go to a different house for each course. This works great for a neighborhood Christmas Party and it takes the burden off of one person, making the party even more fun! Or your party could be for a more specific purpose, such as Christmas caroling, tree-trimming, exchanging Christmas cookies, writing Christmas cards, making Christmas gifts, wishing Jesus "Happy Birthday," or even visiting a homeless shelter or nursing home.

Why do we have Christmas Parties?

• Parties are a great opportunity to bring family, friends, and associates together.

• They're an opportunity to "give back" to those who have given to us all year.

• We're able to get together, relax, and talk with those we care about.

• Christmas Parties are fun.

• We have them for the memories.

• They're a good excuse to be with people you haven't seen for years.

• We want to have family and friends over to enjoy our home and Christmas decorations.

- We enjoy watching our children get excited.
- Christmas Parties give children good experiences and a sense of tradition, leading to security and comfort.
- We have a reason to clean the house!
- Why not?

How do you get started?

Start with a plan, early so you can enjoy your party, both the preparation and the giving. Then take one step at a time:

1. Determine the purpose of your party and pick a theme for it from this book. A theme gives you direction: It's like a roadmap, helping you know where you're going. It also helps your guests since they'll know what to wear and what to expect. First, figure out the purpose of your party: Is it a children's school party, a Christmas cookie exchange, dinner with friends or family? Or is it for making crafts to give as gifts, wrapping presents for the disadvantaged, sewing Christmas stockings, or just plain having fun?

Then pick a theme for your Christmas Party. For example, Santa and His Elves is a popular theme for a family party, especially when you include a visit from the Jolly Old Elf himself. A natural combination is to add Rudolph and His Reindeer as a second theme. Do a craft and activity from one theme, and have drinks and goodies from the other.

2. Identify your age group. Will the party be for adults, children, or both?

3. Make your guest list. Give this some thought. Invite people that mean something to you, or you think would get along well together.

4. Decide on a *formal or informal party.* This will determine things such as place settings, seating requirements, and attire.

5. Set a date, and send your invitations well in advance, whether written, by phone, or e-mail. Give two to three weeks notice for this time of year. People's calendars fill up fast and they have extra chores with shopping and baking. Ask them to R.S.V.P. but be prepared for cancellations due to weather, flu and cold season, and busy schedules.

6. Decide on the time and the length of your party. A party for children is probably best in the afternoon, and for no longer than 3 hours, but it depends on the age group, number of children, and your stamina. An adult party is easier in the evening and can last 3 to 5 hours. If you're including both adults and children, the purpose of your party will help determine the time of day. For example, if it's a caroling party, evening is traditional. But if it's to visit a nursing home and hand out gifts, you should go in the afternoon.

Tell us about a favorite holiday memory. "People always ask me if the character of the Great Aunt in A Cup of Christmas Tea is based upon an actual relative of mine because she seems so real on the page. She is indeed based upon both of my grandmothers, who both made Christmas come alive for our family. Their Christmas tables were laden with all wonders that butter, sugar, flour, eggs, and imagination could possibly yield. My favorites were "Berlinerkranz"— those superbuttery spritz cookies crowned with rock sugar and done in the shape of wreaths. There was also a meatball soup, with clear amber broth that fairly exploded with the deepest and most profound flavors. They invested vast amounts of time in preparation, and their love for us was made manifest always through what they did for us all, day by day and season after season."
—Tom Hegg
Author of A Cup of Christmas Tea and its sequel, the just-released A Memory of Christmas Tea

Whatever your decision, always plan the first half hour for waiting for people to arrive, greeting them, taking their coats, offering them drinks, showing them around, and introducing them to others. You'll need 15 minutes at the end of the party for your guests to gather up personal belongings and say their good-byes. So far, your party is 45 minutes. Now estimate a time for each activity. For example, two games could add 30 to 45 minutes. If you plan a gift exchange for about a dozen people, plan on 30 minutes. A buffet dinner takes 30 minutes tops. Then 15 minutes for dessert and coffee and people are ready to go. You can see that a party can easily take 2 hours.

You may want to point out a specific time for an event on your invitations in case some guests will be arriving late due to other commitments, such as "Santa arrives at 8:00 pm." Be sure to state an ending time on the invitation to give people an idea when the party will be over, or when they need to pick up their children.

7. Next *find a place*, especially if your home is out of the question. Ask yourself, is your home big enough? If so, are there certain rooms off-limits? Do you have any pets that may cause a problem? Will you need a babysitter for your children or other people's? Do you have enough parking? Can people find your house, or will they need a map?

If your house is out, where else could you have a party? Do you have a clubhouse in your neighborhood you can use? If so, will you need to pay a fee, put a deposit down for cleaning, or sign a contract? Is there a kitchen, pots, pans, and utensils? Are there chairs, tables, even toilet paper? Does the clubhouse have enough outlets, or will you need to bring extension cords? Is there heat? How many people will it safely hold? These are just some of the questions you'll want to ask. I'm sure you'll have some of your own.

If your house is too small, and you don't have a clubhouse, perhaps you can rent a hall. But if that's too expensive, you may be able to use the office, the church, or your child's school. Or a relative with a larger house may very well enjoy helping you host your party. I have a friend who used her cousin's party room in her downtown apartment building. Not only were the guests thrilled with the prospect, but the view was magnificent.

8. Make a list of *what you need for your party*. This book will help you with its supply list for each game, craft, and goody. Other items to include are plates, napkins, utensils, cups, ice, bottle openers, towels for spills, and trashcans, even recycling bins clearly marked if you're so inclined. You will need a good location to serve food and drinks, even if that entails a help-yourself table or counter, and someplace for your guests to put their things, whether those are coats, purses, boots, or gifts. You may want to have a camera or two handy, and music all ready to go. Most important, have some flexibility so you and your guests will have fun.

9. Just as there are several things you want at your party, there are *things you don't want:* too much of the same kind of food, like sweet or salty; too much of just one drink—have an assortment—some people may just want water; or even too many activities.

10. Now that you have a plan, *write a schedule:*
    - Four weeks before the party, prepare a guest list, decide on a date, time, and place, and choose a theme. Invite your guests.
    - Three weeks before, pick games and prizes, crafts or favors, food, drinks, and decorations. Start shopping for hard-to-find items.
    - Two weeks before, finish your shopping, other than for fresh food, and do any early preparations you can, such as for games, crafts, or favors.
    - One week before, confirm any bookings for a clubhouse or hall and entertainment, call those who haven't R.S.V.P.'d, and check to see if you need film or batteries for your still and video cameras.
    - Two days before, clean the house, or at least the area you'll have the party including the guest bathroom. Review all your notes to be sure you have everything. Make a list of any last-minute items you need to purchase.
    - One day before, do the last-minute shopping for fresh food and things you've overlooked. Prepare any food or drink that can be done ahead, or needs to be refrigerated for a day.
    - The day of the party, decorate the party area, set up tables and chairs, and put out any prizes or items for games and crafts. Make the food and drinks.
    - One hour before your guests arrive, try to have everything done, including "yourself," then sit, relax, and review your notes. You may have forgotten something and you may still have time to do it.
    - When guests start arriving, be sure to take their coats, put any food or gift items where they go, give them any needed instructions, introduce them around, and make them feel at home.
    - HAVE FUN!

Handing Out Prizes

If you're having a school, church, or youth party outside of your home, one issue you need to address is handing out prizes or favors. Do you want everyone scattering from the game area to put away their prizes at their desks or with their coats? Or worse, do you want to lose their attention when they unwrap, eat, or start playing with their prizes. Be prepared to deal with the situation beforehand. For example, allow 5 minutes until you start a new game if you want them to put their prizes away. Take into consideration the ages in the group when choosing favors, and be sure to have at least one for every young child, and extra in case of breakage. Also, remember the diversity issue in some groups.

Share an idea for a gift you gave someone that took time and creativity. "My husband and I built boxes for our children with locks for their memories."
—Vickie Christiansen
Potsdam, New York

What was the best Christmas gift you received as a child? Why? What age were you? "A train. My dad was in the war and my Uncle Paul gave me everything he gave his own son. I was five or six."
—Rudy Savage
Golden, Colorado

What has been your most favorite thing to do at Christmas? "Opening presents with the family and seeing their expression when they open my gifts, which I bought with my own money."
—Rom Savage, Age 15
Golden, Colorado

Stress at Christmastime

Yes, there is stress around the Christmas holiday season. It's hard not to escape it, what with Christmas cards, decorating the house and tree, gift shopping, baking, and extra social, church, and school functions added to our already busy lives.

True, you may no longer try to do it all, for example, you may not be into making Christmas cookies or you decided long ago to stop sending Christmas cards. But your schedule may be just as full. Perhaps you work outside the home, or you're a stay-at-home mom who loves to volunteer. It doesn't matter. There's no getting around it. This is an extra busy time of year for everyone.

Here are some suggestions to help you reduce the stress so you can focus on the fun part of the holidays—PARTIES:

- Early in November, spend a few hours to gather your thoughts and write down what things you need or want to do for the holidays. Include a shopping list of those you want to give gifts to, along with ideas for them. Jot down stores, catalogs, or Internet sites you will want to browse.

- Note how you would like to decorate the house and tree, and any items you'll need to purchase. You may want to do an inventory of your decorations first. Since you have everything out of storage, why not start decorating, making it a goal to have it all done by Thanksgiving? Or take out last year's pictures to help trigger your memory.

- Then start your shopping and avoid the times the stores are the busiest. I have found that the first and last hours stores are open are when they are the least crowded.

- Wrapping all the gifts at the same time also saves wear and tear on your schedule.

- To save some time on Christmas cards, get a family picture taken early or use a picture from your summer vacation—maybe the family at the beach in swimming suits and Santa hats (if you were thinking ahead). Order them as soon as they are offered in the stores, pay the extra dollars to have them personalized with your signature, and use self-adhesive address labels, a sure time-saver. No, it's not as personal, but at least you're sending something. Children can help with stuffing the envelopes and putting on stamps. Make a game of it. Play Christmas music and race to the finish, neatly of course.

- You'll also want to start baking and freezing cookies or quick breads early. Use freezer bags or good plastic containers to avoid freezer burn. On a cold day in September or October, the oven will warm up the kitchen and you won't have to turn on the heat.

- After Christmas, write down things you'd like to do next year and keep it somewhere you'll be able to find it, perhaps taped to the month of November in your new calendar. Works for me.

- And be sure to get extra rest, exercise, and good nutrition to stay healthy so you'll enjoy all the parties when it's that time.

A little bit of organization can go a long way when it comes to the Christmas holiday season. Following the above steps will leave you less stressed and a lot more able to enjoy Christmas Parties, not to mention your friends, your family, and the big day itself!

Ways others eliminate stress

As you can see, you too can survive having a Christmas Party. It doesn't need to be stressful. Here are some ways other people say they eliminate stress during the holidays:

 "Watch National Lampoon's Christmas Vacation."
— Richard L. Dmytryshyn, Colorado

 "Start early; plan out your days; make lists."
—Danielle Dell, California

 "No doubt it was the Christmas Eve my son was six years old. The kids were in bed and I was peeking in their rooms to see if they were asleep. Christmas morning, my son was ecstatic as he ran into our room and told us he saw Santa peeking in his room the night before! Suddenly it hit me, Christmas Eve I was wearing a white-collared, red velour robe. It was by far the sweetest, magical Christmas memory."
—Renee Zumpano, Akron, Ohio

 "Shop all year round instead of at the last minute."
—Margaret Ripple, Indiana

 "My friends have Christmas on January 1, making December 25 strictly devoted to remembering Christ's birth."
—Vickie Christiansen, New York

 "Number one motto: less is more. Involve the family as much as possible; prepare meals and dishes in advance and freeze them."
—Nancy Savage, Colorado

 "Save some vacation days to do shopping and family stuff without being rushed."
—Jeff Hill, Ohio

"I go on a short trip with my best friends. I go somewhere with a lot of nature so that I forget my daily life. I often visit the hot springs and take a bath, have a gorgeous dinner, and talk all night with my friends."
—Masako Matsumoto, Japan

"Downsize on gifts. Also make homemade gifts. For example, jams and jellies during the summer to save for Christmas gift giving. Top the jars with holiday fabric and bows. Make plenty so you always have a gift on hand for those who stop by [or when you're invited to a party] during the holidays. You can enjoy any leftovers throughout the winter."
—MaryAnn Stevens, Michigan

 "Go for long walks outside with someone you love."
—Shalaine Root, Colorado

What part of the holiday do you enjoy the most? Why?
"Going to church at midnight with my whole family, It gives me a sense of piece."
—Henrietta Matteucci San Jose, California

What family traditions do you have for the holidays?
"Christmas Eve we dress-up and have dinner OUT!!"
—Hazel O'Meara Denver, Colorado

What is a good Christmas gift? What was the best gift you ever gave?
"A donation to a cat shelter in the name of 'someone in our family who had everything' because she loves cats."
—Shalaine Root Thornton, Colorado

17

Christmas Stores, Tell Us Your Thoughts

Tell us about your most memorable Christmas customer and why?

"One Christmas Eve, a gentleman called to ask if we would stay open—he was just a few minutes away. He raced in about 6 pm, near closing time, and said they were just about to sit down to Christmas Eve dinner and his little boy, age 4 or 5, realized they had no Christmas crackers. He had to find them, because they could not start dinner without them. Of course we stayed open."
—Mary Muszak and Russell Steven,
Owners, Christmas on the Beach
Toronto, Canada

"The first year my shop was open, a woman came flying in about noon, a week before Christmas. She hurriedly began choosing several items, including an 8-foot completely decorated tree, garland, a wreath, and a centerpiece, and wanted them all delivered by 4 pm that afternoon, in time for her party at 5!"
—Jan Tharaldson
Owner, Wind River Silks
Anchorage, Alaska

"Those frantic husbands rushing in the last half of the day on Christmas Eve to purchase collectibles that their wives have been wanting!"
—Shelley Graham
Sales Associate, Samoa
Christmas Wreath Gift Shop
Samoa, California

"A gentleman and his family were visiting Williamsburg for the holidays from California. He decided it wouldn't be Christmas without the tree and decorations so he called and asked if our shop could come and decorate their hotel suite for Christmas, which we did. Christmas is all about families, love, and children!"
—Sheila Yeatts
Store Manager,
The Chistmas Mouse
Williamsburg, Virginia

"Years ago, a lady came into our shop just before going out to dinner. She selected a small tree and asked if we could put some decorations on it and she'd come back later and buy it. While she was gone, we completely decorated it with an assortment of ornaments we thought she might choose. When she returned, she loved the tree and bought it just as we had done it. She then explained that she had been diagnosed with cancer the previous Christmas and was a survivor! She and her party had come specifically to shop in our store and dine in town."
—Alice Miller
Owner, Christmas Manor
Bryan, Ohio

"One Christmas season, we shipped fifty-eight fully decorated Christmas trees to a chain of restaurants in Japan via air cargo. Through the years, Lance and MaryAnn Williams of Rome, New York, have purchased numerous trees and ornaments and now display all their ornaments on twenty-five trees for their community to view at an annual open house. We have supplied Christmas decorations for movie sets including Shaft, Jingle all the Way, Frost, Enemy of The State, Must Be Santa, Simple Plan, The Grinch, and Riding in Cars with Boys. But on December 15, 1976, we were thrilled to receive a phone call from John Wayne. 'This is the Duke calling,' he said. 'I have been told that BRONNER'S CHRISTmas WONDERLAND has the best selection of Santa suits. Can you supply one for me, and how fast can you ship it because I need it to play a Santa helper at a Christmas party?'"
—Wally Bronner
Originator, BRONNER'S
CHRISTmas
WONDERLAND
World's Largest
Christmas Store
Frankenmuth, Michigan

"Every year, all our stores do displays using Department 56®, Inc. village pieces. I created a wreath using the Custom Stitchers piece. Along with the house, it had scissors, a tape measure, pins, buttons, and thread, etc.—things I brought from home for ideas. A fellow came along and wanted to purchase it for his wife, a 'stitcher' herself, no matter what the cost, as his wife was dying of cancer. It gave me a good feeling that I created something that gave pleasure to someone on her last holiday season."
—Susan Mead
Store Manager, World of Christmas
Park Rapids, Minnesota

Does your store have a motto?

"Enjoy CHRISTmas, it's HIS Birthday; Enjoy LIFE, it's HIS way."
—Wally Bronner
Originator,
BRONNER'S
CHRISTmas
WONDERLAND
World's Largest
Christmas Store,
Frankenmuth,
Michigan

What have been some of the more popular Christmas/ holiday trends or traditions in your region?

"The holiday trend in Westmont is putting up elaborate outdoor Christmas decorations, lighting, and commercial animations. We have contests and awards and scheduled bus tours so everyone can enjoy the decorations. The Chicago area is known as the 'decorating capital of the world.'"
—**Roger Farrow**
Owner, Holiday Displays, Inc.
Westmont, Illinois

"I was surprised at how upscale, contemporary, and in tune with current trends my clientele in Anchorage was when compared to clients in the Seattle area. I think because my customers are well-traveled and have moved around a lot with the oil industry. The trends are not the Alaskan, rustic themes I expected but the bright vibrant colors—jewel tones. In fact the chartreuse and plum color schemes were the first to sell out!"
—**Jan Tharaldson**
Owner, Wind River Silks
Anchorage, Alaska

"Collecting the old traditional glass from Germany is a popular trend and it keeps growing each year. Also, nativity sets are very popular, especially for families with very young children."
—**Mary Muszak and Russell Steven,**
Owners, Christmas on the Beach
Toronto, Canada

"In October in Morro Bay, we have our annual Harbor Festival with all kinds of arts and crafts, wines, and seafood. The first Saturday in December, there is the lighted boat parade. The residents go all out to decorate their boats with Santas, snowmen, and all kinds of Christmas lights. They put them in the water and go back and forth in the harbor for a 2-hour nighttime parade."
—**Sharon Reynolds**
Store Manager,
Forever Christmas
Morro Bay, California

"Woodstock, in the foothills of the Catskills, is like the crossroads of the world. People from all over visit. Trends among the locals seem to be toward Christmas elegance—lots of bows, frills, and lots of gold and crystal. My customers are looking for a change, a new theme to their decorating—traditional but elegant. A post World War II tradition continues on Christmas Eve, when Santa Claus arrives in town in a new unique way. He has come by camelback, sky crane, hot air balloon, and this year riding in a 1918 Oldsmobile through a tunnel, appearing on the other side in a DeLorean! Every year it's different. There are some 4,000 people on the green, singing, waiting in anticipation of Santa's arrival."
—**Mark Hedrick**
Owner,
Holiday Haus of Woodstock
Woodstock, NY

"We have a resident rooster in the shop—everyone comes to see him. In Samoa, we have winter festivals that include traditions of the Native American population in our area. Current trends in ornaments seem to be old-fashioned hand-blown glass, penguins, angels, and bright colors. Lighthouses and shell ornaments are especially popular with our summer tourists."
—**Shelley Graham**
Sales Associate, Samoa
Christmas Wreath Gift Shop
Samoa, California

"Each year, 2 million guests and customers come to us from around the world to inspect our 750 nativity scenes and 10,000 ornaments. Parents and children visit to select one or more favorite ornaments. Often, parents make a list of each child's selections. At the time of the child's wedding, the parents make a present of all the ornaments selected throughout the years."
—**Wally Bronner**
Originator, BRONNER'S CHRISTmas WONDERLAND
World's Largest Christmas Store
Frankenmuth, Michigan

"Our town celebrates 'Nights Before Christmas' at Memorial Hall Center for the Arts with displays of all kinds of decorated trees (sponsored by individuals and businesses), concerts, and other events."
—**Marianne and Jack Kipnes**
Owners, The Christmas Barn
Wilmington, Vermont

"The biggest event in Williamsburg for the holidays is the 'Grand Illumination' on the first Sunday of December. This is when Colonial Williamsburg is lit up—all the windows in the entire town have brass candleholders with white candles, which are a symbol of welcome and hospitality. Some homes and businesses keep their candles lit year round. We complete the celebration with fireworks and fife and drum. Another tradition is decorating with lots of fruit (especially apples), holly and berries, pinecones, and big red bows on wreaths, garland, and trees."
—**Sheila Yeatts**
Store Manager,
The Chistmas Mouse
Williamsburg, Virginia

Is there anything special your stores have done for the holidays?

"In November ever year, we have an open house and serve our own homemade fudge and hot cider. Last year, all four stores collected donations from new 'beanies' and the customers chose an organization, such as the Salvation Army, a hospice, or a crisis center, for their donation to go from the sale."
—**Susan Mead**
Store Manager,
World of Christmas
Park Rapids, Minnesota

"In all six stores, we have fifty trees, each decorated in a different theme from cartoon characters to Victorian elegance."
—**Sheila Yeatts**
Store Manager,
The Chistmas Mouse
Williamsburg, Virginia

See additional interviews from Christmas Stores on pages 25 and 30.

CHAPTER 2
Games

Helpful Hints for Games

1. Read the supply list, as some of the games require preparation beforehand.

2. Make adjustments for handicapped or much younger children, such as moving the starting line for tossing games. Or allow them more time to play.

3. In other books in the **What Do I Do?**® series, we make a starting line with masking tape, but you can substitute other items such as a yardstick or piece of rope.

4. Always explain the object of the game, even obvious ones like Pin the Nose on Rudolph, found on page 46.

5. Games that require retrieval of balls, candy, or other items will run better if there are two people to go after them.

6. If you can, give out prizes. Be sure to give something to "losing" team members or individual players. This can be as small as a piece of candy.

7. For unique prizes, crack open walnuts and insert special Christmas messages.

8. Any game that calls for stockings means Christmas stockings, unless otherwise specified.

9. We have added some twists to certain games in the Christmas Here, There, and Everywhere—Global Celebrations chapter, so they may not be played exactly the way they are in their countries of origin.

10. If you live in a warm climate, most of the games can be played outside. Or children and adults can dress in winter gear to pretend it's a snowy, cold, winter day.

11. Keep all games and prizes safe for children.

12. Limit games to 5 minutes long for younger children.

13. Allow approximately 20 minutes to play games that include relays or lots of people.

14. When a game calls for teams and you have only enough people for one team, play against the clock instead.

15. Be flexible. If a game is not working well, stop playing it and start a different one.

16. Have a game in reserve in case the above happens, or the games you've planned go faster than you expected. Good backups are Hidden Christmas Words, found on page 171, or Christmas Word Search, found on page 172.

17. Have something to do for children that get eliminated from a game, such as MistleTOES, found on page 170. An older child or adult will be happy to supervise.

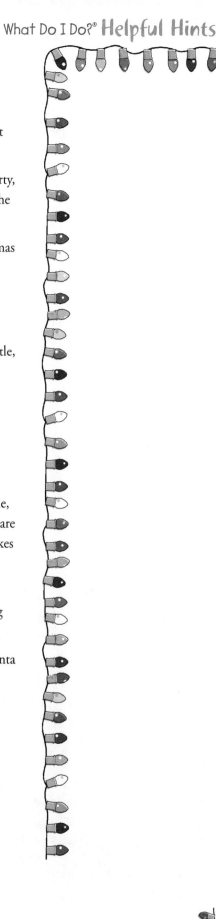

18. Keep in mind that some people may not want to play games but make great spectators. Ask them to cheer for their friends and family members.

19. If you have more than one game going at the same time, like at a school party, have all the games equal in length. This will allow the stations to rotate at the same time.

20. If a station has finished its game before the others, read some of the Christmas educational facts to them found in the sidebars of this book.

21. A rotation of four games works best for any age level.

22. Try to have an adult at each station.

23. Have one person tell the groups when to rotate. He can do this with a whistle, by turning the lights off and on, or hollering "Ho! Ho! Ho!"

24. Listen to Christmas music while playing your games.

25. Some games can be made into stocking stuffers.

26. Take time to play any games you've received as Christmas presents.

27. Parents, this is a good game for you. When you put the names on your children's presents, put the wrong names on them but don't tell. For example, if you have three children—Dom, Sam, and Willie—all presents for Dom are marked for Willie, Willie's say Sam, and Sam's say Dom. See how long it takes your children to catch on!

28. A great tradition is to drive around and look at Christmas lights. Record where you've seen the best ones and take the list with you every year, adding to it.

29. Remember, one of the best activities for a Christmas party is a visit from Santa Claus.

30. Have Santa join in on any games.

What do you remember best about Christmas as a child?

"Those first magical moments when you wake up, remember it's Christmas morning, then go down-stairs to the tree and see all those beautiful packages under the tree that's been lit, and there's Christmas music on the stereo."

—Pamela Kennedy
Plum, Pennsylvania

Decorate the Tree

Supplies

Scissors
Green poster board
Yellow poster board
Glue
Masking tape
Twelve different wrapped candies (per player)

Directions

1. Cut out a large Christmas tree from the green poster board.

2. Cut a star from the yellow poster board and glue it to the top of the tree.

3. Lay the tree on the floor and make a starting line with the masking tape about 5 feet away.

4. To play the game, give the players twelve different wrapped candies each and have them, one at a time, stand behind the starting line to toss their candies onto the tree. Each candy represents an ornament.

5. Score one point for each ornament on the tree. If one ornament pushes another one off, it doesn't count. Highest score wins.

Tip: Adjust the starting line for younger children. If adults are playing, have two starting lines—one closer for children.

Note: Flat candy works better for younger children. Round or irregular shaped candies may roll off the tree. Use them for older children or adults.

Christmas Trees, Stockings, and Candy Canes

Human Christmas Tree

Supplies

Pencils

Scissors

White poster board

Glue

Silver glitter

Paper hole puncher

Brown pipe cleaner

Headband

Two short stools

Chair

Five children dressed in green clothes

Five Christmas songbooks

Directions

1. Draw and cut out a 5-inch star from the white poster board.

2. Glue and glitter one side of the star. Let it dry.

3. Punch a hole in the bottom two points of the star.

4. Cut the pipe cleaner in half. Thread one half through one hole of the star and wind it around the headband, the other half through the other hole and around the headband. The star will stand straight up. Adjust if needed.

5. Place one stool on each side of the chair.

6. Have one child sit on the floor next to the stool on the left, and one on the right. Then have one child sit on each stool and one on the chair. Follow the illustration so the children's positions form a tree.

7. The child on the chair wears the star headband.

8. Give each child a songbook to sing Christmas carols.

Is there anything special your stores have done for the holidays?
"In 1992, Bronner's erected an authorized replica of the Silent Night Memorial Chapel in Oberndorf/Salzburg, Austria, as a tribute of thankfulness to God from Wallace and Irene Bronner and family. The memorial chapel is open daily for visitation and meditation. Wally Bronner was thrilled to present one verse of 'Silent Night' (the world's favorite Christmas carol) in over 300 languages to the Silent Night Museum/ Oberndorf, during a December 11, 1999, symposium in Wagrain, Austria."

—Wally Bronner
Originator, BRONNER'S
CHRISTMAS WONDERLAND
World's Largest
Christmas Store
Frankenmuth, Michigan

Presents Under the Tree

Supplies

Two items from around the house per player, the same amount and similar for each team (for example, for two teams, two pair of slippers for Mom, two ties for Dad, two bottles of perfume for sister Victoria, two toys for baby Alex, and so on; for three teams, three pair of slippers and so on)

All the following per team:

Large roll of Christmas gift wrap

Ball of string

Package of ¾-inch colored round labels, self-adhesive

Bag of rubber bands, assorted sizes

Roll of curling ribbon

Bag of bows

Paper

Pen

Scissors

Tape

Christmas music

Directions

1. The object of the game is for teams to wrap their presents and put them under the tree. One adult will need to judge the teams by the rules in step #5.

2. Determine how many players you will have and how big you want your teams. Choose gifts from around the house accordingly, two per player but the same amount and similar for each team. Make a gift list of the items you're using and whom they are for, such as slippers for Mom, tie for Dad, toy for baby Alex, and so on. Make one copy per team.

3. Lay the presents to be wrapped by each team with a gift list, gift wrap, string, labels, rubber bands, curling ribbon, bows, paper, and a pen.

4. Let each team choose to add either scissors or tape to their pile to use for wrapping its gifts. *It can't have both.*

5. Here are the rules and point value to give to the judge and read to the teams before starting:

Rule 1. Gifts must be wrapped neatly and held together with one or more of the following items: string, labels, rubber bands, and tape, if you have it.

Rule 2. Each gift must have curling ribbon and a bow on it.

Rule 3. You will need to have a gift label (made from paper) on each present, which has the person's name, what the gift is, and a rhyme to go with it. Here's an example:

Dad, here's a hammer,
Now fix your grammar.

Your rhyme has to be at least two lines.

Scores will be determined as follows:

1–10 points for how well your team works together.

1–5 points for how neat your packages are wrapped.

1–5 points for how creatively your presents are wrapped.

1–5 points for how cool your rhymes are.

1–20 points for how well your team follows directions.

Bonus of 10 points to the team that finishes wrapping all its presents first.

Bonus of 1 point for each gift under the tree.

6. On "Go," start the Christmas music for the teams to start wrapping their gifts. When they finish each one, they should put it under the tree, in the team's own pile.

Tip: This game can go long, so if you're limited on time, choose one present per player or set a time limit of 20 minutes.

Note: Add any other rules you want such as no pushing or yelling.

What's your favorite Christmas book or story? "A special story written by a friend about my brother who died."
—Vickie Christiansen
Potsdam, New York

Christmas Tree Stories

Supplies — none

Directions

There are two variations for playing this game:

Variation 1: Have players choose an idea from those listed below. Give them five minutes to make up a short story they will tell to the group.

- You are a Christmas tree in a Christmas tree lot. Families are there searching for the perfect tree. If you could talk, what would you tell them?

- You are a Christmas tree—if you could give yourself a name what would it be and why?

- The family has just started to decorate you, a Christmas tree. What suggestions could you give them?

Variation 2: Use an idea for a story from the above list. Designate a person to be the leader. Have him or her choose one player to begin the story. When the leader points to another player, that player continues telling the story, and so on.

Stocking Stuffer Relay

Supplies

One large stocking (per team)

Stocking stuffers (same for each team and enough to overfill stockings)

Variation: Pillows

Directions

1. Divide the players into equal teams.

2. Hang each stocking on a hook or chair at least 10 feet away from the teams.

3. Place the same amount and identical stocking stuffers on the floor next to each team.

4. On the word "Go," the first player in each team will choose any item from his team's pile, run over to his team's stocking, and stuff the item in the stocking. He then runs back and tags the next player on his team, who chooses any item from the pile and stuffs it in the stocking and so on.

5. First team to fill its stocking with all its items wins. Let each team divide its stocking stuffers among itself to keep.

Variation: As an obstacle, place a couple of pillows between each team and its stocking. The players have to jump over the pillows both ways.

Miniature Stocking Hunt

Legend says there were three sisters who after washing their stockings, hung them to dry by the fireplace. A man named Nicholas tossed three bags of gold down the chimney; each fell into a stocking for the girls to use as a dowry.

Supplies

Miniature Christmas stockings (average five per player)

Christmas candy

Money

Numbered pieces of paper (one per stocking)

Presents (one per stocking)

Directions

1. Fill each miniature stocking with candy, money, and a numbered piece of paper.

2. Hide the stockings (count how many) just like you would Easter eggs, easy for the young kids and harder for the older ones.

3. On the word "Go," let the children find the stockings.

4. When all the stockings have been found, have everyone empty their stockings (they get to keep everything) while you set the presents in a row.

5. The child with the first number chooses a present. Then the child with the second number chooses a present and so on.

6. When all the numbers have been turned in, collect the stockings for next year and let the kids swap presents with each other if they want.

Note: If you have good weather, this game is fun to play outdoors.

Decorate the Tree

Scissors
Green poster board
Yellow poster board
Glue
Masking tape
Twelve different
  wrapped candies
  (per player)

Human Christmas Tree

Pencils
Scissors
White poster board
Glue
Silver glitter
Paper hole puncher
Brown pipe cleaner
Headband
Two short stools
Chair
Five children dressed
  in green clothes
Five Christmas
  songbooks

Presents Under the Tree

Two items from around
the house per player,
the same amount and
similar for each team
(for example, for two
teams, two pair of
slippers for Mom,
two ties for Dad, two
bottles of perfume for
sister Victoria, two
toys for baby Alex, and
so on; for three teams,
three pair of slippers
and so on)

All the following
  per team:
Large roll of Christmas
  gift wrap
Ball of string
Package of ¾-inch
  colored round labels,
  self-adhesive
Bag of rubber bands,
  assorted sizes
Roll of curling ribbon
Bag of bows
Paper
Pen
Scissors
Tape
Christmas music

Christmas Tree Stories

Stocking Stuffer Relay

One large stocking
  (per team)
Stocking stuffers
  (same for each
  team and enough to
  overfill stockings)
Variation: Pillows

Don't forget the
camera and film

Supplies for Christmas Trees, Stockings, and Candy Canes

Miniature Stocking Hunt

Miniature Christmas
  stockings (average
  five per player)
Christmas candy
Money
Numbered pieces
  of paper (one per
  stocking)
Presents
  (one per stocking)

Blow the Snow Away

Supplies

Table

Two blow dryers

Two trashcans

White paper (at least 100 sheets)

Off-white paper (at least 100 sheets)

Two sheets of newspaper

Directions

1. Place the table so one end is near an outlet to plug in the blow dryers. Divide the players into two teams.

2. Each team is given a shovel (trashcan), equal amount of paper (one team white, the other off-white), and a blow dryer.

3. One player from each team stands 2 feet from the end of the table (opposite the outlet), holding their shovels (trashcans). They must each stand and stay on top of a sheet of newspaper.

4. All the other players stand at the other end of the table with the blow dryers and stacks of paper, opposite their respectful teammates.

5. Have one person on each team be in charge of a blow dryer, and all the others stand in line to the side of the table, near their paper.

6. On the word "Go," the first player of each team crumples a piece of paper to form a snowball and places it on the table.

7. The person with the dryer blows it across the table to his or her teammate who attempts to capture the snowball with the shovel (trashcan). If that player goes off of the newspaper to catch the snowball, that ball will be forfeited.

8. The players need to move quickly after making their snowballs, going to the end of the line while the next players make snowballs, and so on.

9. The winning team is the one who has collected the most snowballs in its shovel (trashcan) when time is called. Play the game for approximately two minutes, or until you have no more paper to make into snowballs.

Note: If there is an odd number of players, one could be a timer or referee.

Variation 1: This game could be played solitaire.

Variation 2: If you have a lot of players and enough supplies, form more teams.

Variation 3: Replay the game, but first rotate the players' positions and uncrumple the paper.

Snow, Snowmen, and Snowflakes

Gotcha!
Indoor Snowball Fight

Supplies

One ream plain white paper
(500 sheets)

Two laundry baskets

Whistle

Notepad

Pencil

Directions

1. Form two teams. Call them the red team and the green team.

2. Give each team one-half ream of paper (250 sheets), and a laundry basket.

3. Each team chooses a home base and takes its paper and basket to it.

4. They crumple their paper into snowballs and put them in their baskets.

5. Choose someone to be the snowball referee. When he blows the whistle, the snowball fight begins. Since he also makes sure the snowball fight stays fair and safe, it's best if the referee is an adult.

6. Choose another adult to be the scorekeeper. He will need to draw two columns on the notepad with the pencil, calling one the red team and the other the green team.

7. When a snowball hits a player, the thrower yells,"Gotcha" and his or her own team's name, for example "Gotcha red team." The scorekeeper then gives a point to the red team, and so on.

Note: To be fair to both teams you must count the paper or give each team its own ream.

Is there anything special your stores have done for the holidays?

"The unique thing about our shop is that we are in an old Victorian home. We completely decorate the home inside and out with lights, trees, flowers, garland, and wreaths (which we design and make). We like to be able to give our customers ideas on how they can decorate as well, so people will see how they might do their homes. We have a snowman tree since snowman ornaments and decorations are our best-sellers."

—Alice Miller
Owner,
Christmas Manor
Bryan, Ohio

Stuff the Snowman

Supplies

Two white sheets

Lots of towels and/or clothes for stuffing

Safety pins

Masking tape

Large belts

Hat for snowman

Scarf

Camera

Directions

1. One child gets to be the snowman. The others will create a snowman using two sheets for the body, and towels and/or clothes to fill the body.

2. They can use safety pins, masking tape, or belts to hold everything together. You may want to choose what the children will use, depending on their age.

3. Explain to them that the child who is the snowman's head is the first snowball of the snowman and to work from the neck down to form the two additional snowballs. They should also not bind the snowman's arms up in the sheets.

4. For final touches, have them add the hat and scarf.

5. Let them take turns being the snowman, and take pictures for them to remember how they looked all fluffy and white.

Yea, It's Snowing

Supplies		
Yardstick or ruler	Scissors	Black poster board
Pencil	22 x 28-inch white poster board	Paper hole puncher
	Stapler	String
		Bag of cotton balls

Directions

1. Measure, mark, and cut out four 3 x 28-inch strips from the white poster board.

2. Take one strip and cut it in half, widthwise; throw one half away and staple the other to the end of a second strip. Form a circle with the strips and staple closed. This is the bottom of a snowman.

3. Take a third strip. Form a circle to make the middle of the snowman, staple it closed, then staple it on top of the first circle, to form a figure eight.

4. Take the last strip. Cut some off the end to form a smaller circle for the head of the snowman. Staple it closed then to the top of the middle part of the snowman.

5. Cut a snowman hat from the black poster board, and staple it to the head.

6. Punch a hole through the top of the snowman's hat, tie a string through it, and hang it from a high place.

7. Give kids cotton balls (snow) to throw through the snowman.

Build a Snowman Christmas Exchange

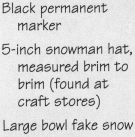

Did you know that most snow falls when it is 15 degrees farenheit and warmer? Colder air doesn't hold as much moisture.

Supplies

- Wrapped gift (one per guest)
- 1-inch mini wooden light bulb
- Orange acrylic paint
- Paintbrush
- Wax paper
- Five ⁷⁄₁₆-inch black buttons with shanks
- Snack-size plastic bags
- Two 25mm moving eyes
- Two 5-inch twigs
- Scissors
- Old glove
- Three ¾-inch red heart buttons
- Knife
- 5-inch Styrofoam® ball
- 6-inch Styrofoam® ball
- 7-inch Styrofoam® ball
- Paper
- Rubber bands
- Pins
- Black permanent marker
- 5-inch snowman hat, measured brim to brim (found at craft stores)
- Large bowl fake snow
- Table and chairs
- Toothpicks
- Foam glue (found at craft stores)

Directions

1. This game is planned for eleven players, but you can adjust it. Read the note at the end to learn how to modify the game for different amounts of people.

2. Ask each guest to bring a wrapped gift. (Decide how much you want them to spend.) The host doesn't bring a gift but supplies all the snowman parts.

3. Paint the mini light bulb orange and lay it on the wax paper to dry.

4. Package the five black buttons in a snack-size plastic bag, the two moving eyes in another plastic bag, and the two twigs in a third bag.

5. Cut two fingers off the glove and put them into a snack-size plastic bag for the snowman's mittens.

6. Finally, package the heart buttons in a plastic bag.

7. Cut a long narrow strip off the glove to become the snowman's scarf.

8. Cut an edge off both sides of the 5 and 6-inch balls. Make sure the 6-inch ball can sit flat on the table. Then cut the edge off one side only of the 4-inch ball. "Stack" the snowman, smallest ball on top. Make sure your cuts are even so the snowman "stacks" well.

9. Put a numbered piece of paper on each of the following eleven items, and secure each with a rubber band or pin, or write on the item with the black permanent marker. Then place each item into the bowl of fake snow. You **must** number the items exactly as follows:

   #1   6-inch Styrofoam® ball

   #2   5-inch Styrofoam® ball

   #3   4-inch Styrofoam® ball

   #4   twigs

   #5   moving eyes

   #6   nose

   #7   black buttons

   #8   red heart buttons

   #9   scarf

   #10 mittens

   #11 snowman hat

10. You are now ready to play the game. Place the toothpicks, foam glue, and bowl of fake snow with the snowman parts on the table. Have the guests take one snowman part each and place their wrapped gifts on the table. There will be one guest without a snowman part who will be the last player. Everyone sits around the table.

11. The player with the #1 snowman part, the 6-inch Styrofoam® ball, goes first. He starts building the snowman by placing his Styrofoam® ball on the table. Then he chooses a gift from the pile, opens it up, and places it in front of him.

12. The player with the #2 snowman part takes his turn by placing toothpicks in the large Styrofoam® ball and attaching the 5-inch Styrofoam® ball to it. Then he decides if he would like to steal #1's gift or choose a gift from the pile. If he steals #1's gift, the first player chooses another gift from the pile.

13. Play continues with #3 placing more toothpicks in his Styrofoam® ball and attaching it on top of the others. The game continues with each player attaching his part to the snowman, using the glue on the table if necessary, and choosing or stealing a gift.

14. The last player can choose to steal a gift, or take the finished snowman. (But the snowman is so cute, you won't want him to leave your house.) Player #1 gets one additional turn to steal from someone since he never had the opportunity. At this point, the game ends. Everyone gets to keep his or her gift, or swap it with someone else.

Note1: Put more or less snowman parts in the plastic bags for different amounts of players.

Note 2: This is a popular game with a snowman twist, so you may prefer to play without the snowman.

Variation 1: Before the game starts decide on how many times a gift can be stolen. Lots of people feel three times is fair. There is always going to be that favorite gift that everyone wants—remember that and bring it next year. You'll be the hit of the party.

Variation 2: Instead of guests buying gifts, ask them to bring something they own that they don't want anymore. We had a yogurt maker exchanged year after year at our neighborhood party, and some great laughs.

We asked 100 people to name their favorite Christmas songs. Here are the results, from most popular to those that received one "vote":

18 Jingle Bells
12 White Christmas
11 Jingle Bell Rock
9 Silent Night
6 Rudolph the Red-Nosed Reindeer
5 Frosty the Snowman
5 The Twelve Days of Christmas
4 Joy to the World
4 Little Drummer Boy
3 Angels We Have Heard On High
3 O Come All Ye Faithful
2 Carol of the Bells
2 Grandma Got Run Over by a Reindeer
2 I Saw Mommy Kissing Santa Claus
2 Winter Wonderland
1 Away in a Manger
1 Do You Hear What I Hear
1 Hark the Herald Angels Sing
1 Holly Jolly Christmas
1 I'm Your Angel
1 Let It Snow! Let It Snow! Let It Snow!
1 Rockin' Around the Christmas Tree
1 Santa Baby
1 The First Noel
1 God Rest Ye Merry Gentlemen
1 O Holy Night
1 Up on the Housetop

The Mitten Exchange

Supplies

Pair of mittens
(one per player)

Small gift
(one per player)

Clothesline

Table and chairs

Christmas music
(one song per
player)

Stereo to play music

Clothespin
(one per player)

Index cards

Pencils (one
per player)

Directions

1. Every guest brings a pair of mittens. Have the guests include a small gift inside one mitten determined by a dollar amount you give them.

2. Set up the clothesline, and the table with the music and stereo. Make sure all the people you've invited can fit around the table.

3. When guests arrive, give them a clothespin and ask them to hang the mitten with the gift on the clothesline. Then have them put the other half of the mitten on the table.

4. When everyone has arrived and all the mittens hung up, you can play the game.

5. Give everyone a pile of index cards and a pencil.

6. To play the game, play a portion of a Christmas song for just a few seconds. The players try to identify the correct name of the song the quickest. Each player writes the name of the song on an index card and slides the card in front of him. You will need to keep track of who put their card out first. If you can work fast enough, number them. (A second person to help you would be great.) Don't be concerned if the guesses are right or not, until everyone's card is on the table.

7. Check #1's card. If the song is correctly identified, full title, he or she is the winner of round one; if not, go to #2's card or #3's or #4's and so on until you find a winner.

8. The winner chooses a mitten from the table, then goes to the clothesline to find the match. They keep the mittens and the gift inside.

9. Play the second round the same way using the back of the index cards, then new index cards for additional rounds. Each winner can continue to play but can't win a mitten again. They may want to just watch. If players are having a hard time guessing the name of a song, play it longer, switch to another song, or give them a clue.

Blow the Snow Away

Table
Two blow dryers
Two trashcans
White paper
   (at least 100
   sheets)
Off-white paper
   (at least 100
   sheets)
Two sheets of
   newspaper

Gotcha! Indoor Snowball Fight

One ream plain
   white paper
   (500 sheets)
Two laundry baskets
Whistle
Notepad
Pencil

Stuff the Snowman

Two white sheets
Lots of towels and/or
   clothes for stuffing
Safety pins
Masking tape
Large belts
Hat for snowman
Scarf
Camera

Yea, It's Snowing

Yardstick or ruler
Pencil
Scissors
22 x 28-inch white
   poster board
Stapler
Black poster board
Paper hole puncher
String
Bag of cotton balls

Don't forget the
camera and film

Supplies for Snow, Snowmen, and Snowflakes

Build a Snowman Christmas Exchange

Wrapped gift
   (one per guest)
1-inch mini wooden
   light bulb
Orange acrylic paint
Paintbrush
Wax paper
Five ⁷⁄₁₆-inch black
   buttons with shanks
Snack-size plastic bags
Two 25mm moving eyes
Two 5-inch twigs
Scissors
Old glove
Three ³⁄₄-inch
   red heart buttons
Knife
5-inch Styrofoam® ball
6-inch Styrofoam® ball
7-inch Styrofoam® ball
Paper
Rubber bands
Pins
Black permanent marker

   (continued)

5-inch snowman hat,
   measured brim to
   brim (found at craft
   stores)
Large bowl fake snow
Table and chairs
Toothpicks
Foam glue (found
   at craft stores)

The Mitten Exchange

Pair of mittens
   (one per player)
Small gift
   (one per player)
Clothesline
Table and chairs
Christmas music
   (one song per player)
Stereo to play music
Clothespin
   (one per player)
Index cards
Pencils
   (one per player)

Shaving Santa's Beard

Supplies

Two chairs

Masking tape

Two Santa hats

Two cans shaving or whipped cream for every six players

One craft stick for every two players

One large towel or barber cape for every two players

One hand towel for every two players

Laundry baskets (enough to hold all the towels/capes)

One small trashcan

Optional: Plastic to cover floor

Directions

1. Divide the players into two teams. Set the chairs on the other side of the room at least 5 feet apart. Use masking tape as the starting line, at least 10 feet from the chairs if possible.

2. Put a Santa hat on each chair. On the floor near each chair, put the following: shaving/whipped cream, craft sticks, large towels/barber capes, and hand towels. Put the laundry basket(s) and the small trashcan between the chairs.

3. With the teams behind the starting line, start the relay. Two players from each team will go at once. One will be Santa, the other the barber.

4. On "Go," four players run down to the chairs, and the Santas sit in the chairs and put their hats on. The barbers drape the large towels/barber capes around the Santas' shoulders, then squirt shaving or whipped cream all over the Santas' faces. Be sure the Santas have their eyes closed and the barbers know that the hair is off-limits.

5. The barbers shave the Santas with the craft sticks, making sure to get all the cream, and then wipe them off with the hand towels. Each pair then throws the hand towel and large towel/barber cape into the laundry basket(s), and the craft stick into the trashcan, then run back to the starting line.

6. The next two players for each team go when the first pair gets back and so on until everyone has had a turn. The first team to finish with clean shaven faces wins. If there is an odd number of players, let someone be a referee.

Optional: Put plastic under the chairs to protect the floors.

Variation 1: Another way to play the game is to have only one pair per team be Santa and the barber with the others cheering.

Variation 2: Or have more chairs and supplies so everyone can play at once.

Pass Santa's Hat, Pass Santa's Gloves, HURRY, HURRY, HURRY!

Supplies

Santa hats
(one per team)

Pillowcases
(one per team)

Gloves
(one pair per team)

Wrigley's 10 PAK,
10 five-stick pack-
ages chewing gum
(one per team)

Directions

1. Put one set of gloves, one Santa hat, and a Wrigley's 10 PAK of gum inside each pillowcase for Santa's toy bag.

2. Divide the players into teams and give the first player on each team a Santa bag.

3. On the word "Go," the first player takes out the Santa hat, puts it on, puts on the gloves, then unwraps the gum package to get one stick out for himself and places it in his mouth. He throws the trash inside the bag.

4. He then takes the gloves and hat off, places them with the gum (not the chewed piece!) back in the bag, and passes everything to the next player on his team.

5. The game continues until all the players have had a turn. First team to finish wins.

Tip: Be sure to have a camera—this game is great for photo shots.

The Undercover Santa

Supplies

Seven to twelve players

Three Santa hats

Chairs for everyone

Two tables

Whistle

Index card and pencil (one per judge)

Directions

1. Choose three players to pretend to be Santa Claus. They will wear the Santa hats, but first need to leave the room.

2. One player needs to be the announcer; all others are the panel of judges.

3. Have the announcer talk to the three Santas, outside the room, to choose who will be the "real" Santa. The announcer explains that the panel of judges will be asking them "yes" or "no" questions. They are to answer the questions how they think the real Santa would answer. An adult may need to supervise this if the players are children.

4. The panel of judges sit at one table opposite the table the Santas will sit. The announcer stands between both tables.

5. When the judges are ready, have the announcer call the Santas into the room and ask them to stand by their chairs. He introduces them as follows: "Number one is Santa Claus, number two is Santa Claus, and number three is Santa Claus. You may all be seated please."

6. Each judge is given one minute to ask any of the three Santas "yes" or "no" questions. The announcer keeps track of the time with the whistle.

7. After each judge is given an opportunity to ask questions, the announcer asks the panel of judges to vote for the "real" Santa. They write their choice of #1, #2, or #3 on their index cards.

8. The announcer asks each judge to show his guess, then asks the "real" Santa to stand.

9. The Santa who believes he answered the questions most realistically stands. More than one may stand so the announcer will again say, "Will the real Santa please stay standing." The Santa who was chosen earlier gets to stay standing.

How Old is Santa?

Supplies		
	Red galoshes (rubber boots)	Red permanent marker
Newspaper	Masking tape	Six ping-pong balls
	White poster board	

Directions

1. Scrunch up newspaper and place in each boot to keep the tops open wide.

2. Place the boots on the floor.

3. With the masking tape, mark a starting line on the floor about 5 feet away from the boots.

4. Tape the white poster board on a wall near the boots. Write at the top: "How Old is Santa?"

5. To play the game, give a player six ping-pong balls, one at a time, to toss into the boots. For every ball he gets into a boot, write "100" on the poster board and say it aloud.

6. Retrieve all the balls and let the next player play, marking 100 on the poster board for each ball in a boot.

7. After all players have had a turn, add up the points to see how old Santa is.

Variation: If you're limited on time or have a large group, you can give the balls to two players, three to each, and let them aim at their own boot. Mark the board, left boot and right boot, and add up the scores for each boot.

HOW OLD IS SANTA?

100
100
100

Feed Santa Cookies and Milk the Fun Way

Supplies

Scissors

Christmas baby bib, bottle, and rattle (per team)

Milk (or drink Santa would like)

Chair (per team)

Plate of two or three Christmas cookies (per team)

Santa hat (per team)

Directions

1. Clean the blades of your scissors. Then slightly cut the tips off the nipples of the bottles so liquid will flow faster through them.

2. Fill each bottle half full of milk (or a drink that Santa would like).

3. Place the chairs on the opposite end of the room with the Santa hats, baby bibs, bottles of milk, rattles, and plates of cookies on the floor next to the chairs.

4. Divide the group into teams and decide who gets to be each team's Santa. Have the Santas sit in their chairs. The rest of the players stand at the opposite end of the room, lined up in their teams.

5. On the word "Go," the first person in line runs to Santa and puts his hat on him, then runs back to the team. The next team member runs to Santa and puts his bib on, then runs back to his team. The next player does the same, giving Santa his rattle. The next player feeds Santa some cookies and milk (not all of it) and runs back. The players after that continue to feed Santa until he has finished all his cookies and milk.

6. When the last player finishes feeding Santa, the player needs to take off his bib, wipe his mouth, and bring everything but Santa back where he started, even his hat. First team back with no milk in its bottle or cookies on its plate wins. No one but "Santa" can have the cookies and milk.

Note: If you play again, first thoroughly wash the bottle and nipple.

Variation: If there are not enough people to race against other teams, play against the clock.

Elf Shoe Toss

Supplies

Scissors
Red poster board
Green poster board

Pencil
Glue gun
Six 1-inch green pom-poms
Six 1-inch red pom-poms

White poster board
Six red pipe cleaners
Six green pipe cleaners
Masking tape

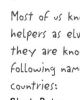

Most of us know Santa's helpers as elves, but they are known by the following names in other countries:

Black Peter – Netherlands,
Knecht Ruprecht Germany, and
Hoesecker – Luxembourg.

Directions

1. Cut out six red and six green 3 x 10-inch rectangles from the poster board.

2. Cut the rectangles (elf shoes) into a point at one short end. Then roll the tips around a pencil very loosely, half the length of the rectangle.

3. At the points, glue the green pom-poms on the red elf shoes and the red pom-poms on the green elf shoes.

4. Glue all the elf shoes on the white poster board a couple of inches apart from each other.

5. Bend the pipe cleaners into circles, twisting the ends together. You will have six red and six green circles.

6. On the curled-up part of the shoes, write elf names. Make up your own or use the following:

Job-sharer Jeffrey
Crafty Cathy
Chisel Charles
Screwdriver Sam
Glueboy Glen
Safety Sheila

Worker Willie
Designer Dolores
Artist Amy

Thinker Tammy
Reader Rose
Painter Peter

7. Mark a starting line on the floor about 5 feet from the elf shoes with the masking tape.

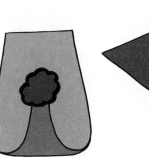 

8. Have each player toss all twelve pipe cleaner circles, one at a time, trying to "ring" the elf shoes.

9. After all the players have had a turn, start over until you run out of time.

Variation: Write the elf names down on paper. As each player tosses the rings, put a checkmark after each elf name whose shoe gets "ringed," to see which elf has the most checkmarks at the end of each round.

Supplies for Santa and His Elves

Shaving Santa's Beard

Two chairs
Masking tape
Two Santa hats
Two cans shaving or
  whipped cream for
  every six players
One craft stick for
  every two players
One large towel or
  barber cape for
  every two players
One hand towel for
  every two players
Laundry baskets
  (enough to hold all
  the towels/capes)
One small trashcan
Optional: Plastic
  to cover floor

Pass Santa's Hat, Pass Santa's Gloves, HURRY, HURRY, HURRY!

Gloves
  (one pair per team)
Santa hats
  (one per team)
Wrigley's 10 PAK,
  10 five-stick packages
  chewing gum (one per
  team)
Pillowcases
  (one per team)

The Undercover Santa

Seven to twelve
  players
Three Santa hats
Chairs for everyone
Two tables
Whistle
Index card and pencil
  (one per judge)

How Old is Santa?

Newspaper
Red galoshes
  (rubber boots)
Masking tape
White poster board
Red permanent
  marker
Six ping-pong balls

Feed Santa Cookies and Milk the Fun Way

Scissors
Christmas baby bib,
  bottle, and rattle
  (per team)
Milk (or drink
  Santa would like)
Chair (per team)
Plate of two or three
  Christmas cookies
  (per team)
Santa hat
  (per team)

Elf Shoe Toss

Scissors
Red poster board
Green poster board
Pencil
Glue gun
Six 1-inch green
  pom-poms
Six 1-inch red
  pom-poms
White poster board
Six red pipe cleaners
Six green pipe
  cleaners
Masking tape

Don't forget the
camera and film

44

The Red Nose Drop

Supplies

Pencil
Paper

Copy machine
Poster board
Scissors
Colored pencils
Red permanent marker

Five white ping-pong balls
Four rolls of toilet paper
Short stool

Directions

1. Trace Rudolph (pattern piece #1) onto the paper, then enlarge it on a copy machine to fit your poster board. Cut it out.

2. Cut the nose out of the poster board, big enough for ping-pong balls to drop through, and color the rest of Rudolph.

3. Use the red permanent marker to completely color all the ping-pong balls.

4. Place the toilet paper rolls on the floor, and lay the poster board on top of them.

5. Place the stool in front of the poster board and have the first player stand on it. Be sure to have a couple spotters in case he should start to fall.

6. Give him five ping-pong balls, one at a time, to drop on the poster, aiming at the nose or where the nose should be. For each ball that goes through the cut-out nose, the player scores 5 points. Have someone ready to retrieve all the balls.

7. The goal is to get all five balls into the nose area (but only one at a time, of course). Five balls multiplied by 5 points equals 25, for Christmas. Yeah!

Note: Each player should keep his elbows tucked into his sides and the ball must be at waist level or higher before dropping it on the poster board.

Variation: Younger children may need to be at ground level to play while older children or adults should be on the stool or higher.

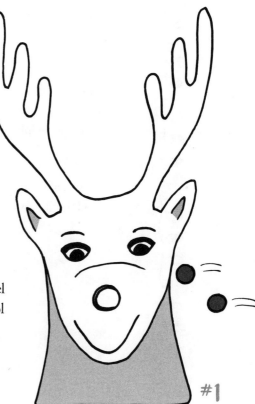

#1

Rudolph and His Reindeer

Pin the Nose on Rudolph

In Clement C. Moore's famous poem, A Visit from Saint Nicholas, he lists eight reindeer names. The reindeer we know today as Donner was written to be "Donder." No one knows how or when the name changed.

What's the best Christmas game you've ever played? "Jesus in the manger adapted from pin the tail on the donkey."
—Melonie R. Ayers
Toledo, Ohio

Supplies

Pencil

Paper

Copy machine

Scissors

Rubber cement

White poster board (choose any size)

Permanent markers (assorted colors)

Masking tape

Reusable adhesive

Large red pom-poms (one per child)

Blindfold

Directions

1. Trace Rudolph (pattern piece #1) onto the paper, then enlarge it on a copy machine to fit your poster board. Cut it out.

2. Quickly brush a layer of rubber cement to the backside of Rudolph and stick it to the poster board.

3. Color Rudolph with the permanent markers, putting an X where his nose should go.

4. Hang Rudolph on a wall with masking tape, about the same height as the children who will play the game.

5. Make a line with masking tape, about 5 to 7 feet away, for the children to stand behind.

6. Place some reusable adhesive onto each pom-pom (for noses).

7. Blindfold the first child, turn him around three times, and have him walk toward Rudolph, directing him if needed. Tell him to place his pom-pom where Rudolph's nose should be.

8. Remove the pom-pom and write the child's name where it was.

9. Have each child take a turn; the nose closest to or hitting the spot where Rudolph's should be wins.

#1

Rudolph Musical Fun

Supplies

Large red pom-poms (one per player)
Rudolph the Red-Nosed Reindeer music
Stereo

Robert L. May, who worked for Montgomery Wards, created and wrote a poem about Rudolph the Red-Nosed Reindeer for a store Christmas promotion. Later, Johnny Marks, Roberts's brother-in-law, wrote the song we all know today. Gene Autry recorded Rudolph the Red-Nosed Reindeer in 1949, selling two million copies.

Directions

1. Give each player a pom-pom and have them stand in a large circle. Tell them the pom-pom is Rudolph's nose.

2. Teach the players the following actions to perform to the corresponding parts of the song. If you don't have a recording, you can always just sing it or have the children and other adults sing along.

When the song says:	What you do:
Rudolph the Red Nosed Reindeer	Put pom-pom on your nose
Other reindeer	Point to others
Shiny nose	Put pom-pom on your nose
Loved	Hug yourself
Shout	Place hands at your mouth like you're shouting
Santa	Put hands in front of your stomach showing a big belly
Guide my sleigh	Sweep hands up to the sky
Laugh	Pretend to laugh
Go down in history	Wiggle down, bent knees, to the ground

3. All other times, have the children just sway back and forth to the music. Play the game several times until everyone has gotten it or wants to stop.

Reindeer Obstacle Course

Supplies

Assorted furniture

Hula-hoop

Reindeer antlers headband (found at party stores or in catalogs)

Blindfold

Video camera

Directions

1. Set up an obstacle course in a large room using furniture and a hula-hoop. Here's an example: a hula-hoop for climbing through (someone needs to hold it up), a stool to jump over, a coffee table to crawl around, and chairs to wind around.

2. Ask who in the group would like to try the obstacle course, and choose one player.

3. Show him the obstacle course and exactly what he'll be doing. Let him try it once. Then take him out of the room, preferably to another part of the house (so he doesn't hear what is happening in the obstacle course room), blindfold him, and put the reindeer antlers headband on him. No, he didn't know he would get blindfolded.

4. While he is gone, the others quietly remove the furniture and items that are part of the obstacle course. When they are finished, they call the player (the reindeer) back to the obstacle course and remind him what he needs to do.

5. On the word "Go," he proceeds to do the obstacle course as he remembers it. Everyone can scream out what actions the player should be doing, like climb through the hula-hoop, wind around the chairs, and so on. It is hysterical to watch as the person tries to do the obstacle course when there is none. Take a video so he can see himself as one of Santa's reindeer.

Note: Once you play this game you can't play it again because people have seen what happens. If you want, you can select a few to do the obstacle course and put them all in a different room and bring one out at a time. But be sure to have them far away from the obstacle course (turn on music or the TV for them) so they don't hear all the laughing.

Tip: Choose anyone with a good personality, who can take kidding, to be the player (the reindeer). Most kids will want to try it.

Mixed-up Reindeer Names

Supplies

Seven index cards (per team)

Scissors

Red permanent marker

Green permanent marker

One envelope (per team)

Optional: Computer and printer, or letter stencil, permanent marker, and card stock

Directions

1. Fold and cut each of the seven index cards into eight square pieces. Discard two squares.

2. Alternate using both permanent markers to write the following reindeer names, one letter from each name per square: Dasher, Dancer, Prancer, Vixen, Comet, Cupid, Donner, Blitzen, and Rudolph. Underline each letter. This will avoid confusion when the letters are mixed-up. For example, an n could look like a u.

4. Count to make sure you have 54 squares with letters on them. Mix them up and put them into an envelope.

5. Repeat steps #1 to #4 for each team.

6. Each team gets an envelope; the first team to spell out all the reindeer names correctly wins.

Note: If the players are young, give them a list of the reindeer names.

Optional: Type the mixed-up reindeer names on the computer or create the cards using a letter stencil, permanent marker, and card stock. You may want to laminate the letters for a game that will last for years.

Antler Toss

Supplies

Twenty-four brown pipe cleaners

Two chairs

Masking tape

Two reindeer antlers headbands (found at party stores or in catalogs)

Directions

1. Take two pipe cleaners and attach them end to end by twisting them together.

2. Bend this long pipe cleaner into a large circle and twist it closed. Make eleven more.

3. Set the chairs about 5 feet from each other and 5 feet from a starting line, made from masking tape.

4. Form two teams. Have one player from each sit in a chair to be a reindeer; the other players stand behind the starting line facing their reindeer teammate.

5. Give the first in line on each team six rings.

6. On the word "Go," the first players toss and try to hook their six rings onto their own reindeer's antlers. They score one point for each ring that stays on the antler.

7. Have a designated player from each team to retrieve the rings and give them to the second player, making sure they get their chance to toss.

8. Play until one team scores 25 points for Christmas Day.

Supplies for Rudolph and His Reindeer

The Red Nose Drop

Pencil
Paper
Copy machine
Poster board
Scissors
Colored pencils
Red permanent
  marker
Five white
  ping-pong balls
Four rolls of
  toilet paper
Short stool

Pin the Nose on Rudolph

Pencil
Paper
Copy machine
Scissors
Rubber cement
White poster board
  (choose any size)
Permanent markers
  (assorted colors)
Masking tape
Reusable adhesive
Large red pom-poms
  (one per child)
Blindfold

Rudolph Musical Fun

Large red pom-poms
  (one per player)
Rudolph the Red-Nosed
  Reindeer music
Stereo

Reindeer Obstacle Course

Assorted furniture
Hula-hoop
Reindeer antlers
  headband (found at
  party stores or in
  catalogs)
Blindfold
Video camera

Mixed-up Reindeer Names

Seven index cards
  (per team)
Scissors
Red permanent
  marker
Green permanent
  marker
One envelope
  (per team)
Optional: Computer
  and printer, or
  letter stencil,
  permanent marker,
  and card stock

Antler Toss

Twenty-four brown
  pipe cleaners
Two chairs
Masking tape
Two reindeer antlers
  headbands (found
  at party stores or
  in catalogs)

Don't forget the
camera and film

The Perfect Snow Angel

Supplies	Two children dressed for snow
	Fresh fallen snow

Directions

1. Have a child, with his arms at his sides and his feet together, fall backward into fresh fallen snow.

2. Tell him to keep his arms straight and drag them up toward his head, then down next to his hips, scraping the snow as he goes.

3. At the same time, have him open and close his legs scissors-style.

4. When he is done forming his angel, have the second child stand at the first child's feet and pull him up by the hands. No hand or footprints from trying to get out of the snow will make The Perfect Snow Angel.

Angel Pick-up Sticks

Supplies	Wax paper
	Red spray paint
Fifty pieces angel hair pasta	Green spray paint

Directions

1. Lay half the pasta on a large sheet of wax paper and the other half on another large sheet. Lightly spray paint one pile of pasta red and the other green. It is important to lightly spray. You do not want the pasta too wet as it will clump. Re-spray a second coat if necessary, then let the pasta dry.

2. Gather up all the pasta "sticks" and mix them up, careful not to break them.

3. To begin play, hold the pasta vertically in the palm of one hand. Keep your hand on the table then quickly let go of the pasta. The pasta will scatter all over the table.

4. Only two people can play at one time. The first player carefully picks up a piece of pasta, red or green, without moving any other pieces of pasta. If he is successful, he continues to pick up pasta the same color. Once he moves any pasta either color while trying to pick up a piece, he needs to leave it.

5. The next player picks up the opposite color unless the first player was unsuccessful in picking up even one piece. Then the second player can go for either color.

6. Continue playing until one player has all twenty-five of his chosen color pasta pieces. He is the winner.

Note: The pasta is fragile and can break easily, so remind the players to be careful.

I Believe in Angels

Angel Bingo

Supplies

White copy paper
Scissors

Mini marshmallows
Bell
Tape

Optional: Garland and glue

Variation: Crayons

An "angel" is not just a heavenly being, but a person who uses his finances to support an enterprise.

Directions

1. Make a copy of the forty-five game pieces (cards with letters and symbols) that are on the following pages. Also, copy the Angel Bingo cards, one per player, and a set of angel wings (pattern piece #1, found on page 63) per game you plan to play (for the winners). Cut out all the game pieces, bingo cards, and angel wings.

2. Choose a dealer/bingo caller and have them shuffle all the game pieces.

3. All the other players get a pile of mini marshmallows (clouds) for markers and one Angel Bingo card. Remind them not to eat the marshmallows until all the games are over unless you have allowed for extras.

   Explain to the players the following:
   • The bingo caller will choose a game piece, show it to everyone, and announce both the letter and the drawing on the piece.
   • The players will put marshmallows (markers) on the area called if it's on their cards.
   • The first player that gets a row covered, either vertically, horizontally, or diagonally should yell "Angel!"

The bingo caller rings the bell each time there is a winner and gives a set of angel wings to him or her. The winners can attach their wings underneath their bingo cards with tape.

Optional: Glue garland on the Angel Bingo cards for angel hair.

Variation: If you feel younger children (or adults) would be better off not having the temptation of marshmallows for markers, use crayons or whatever else works.

A	N	G	E	L
Snowflake	Christmas Tree	Praying Hands	Drummer Boy	Letters to Santa
Angel	Elf	Jingle Bells	Happy New Year	Gingerbread Men
Baby Jesus, Mary and Joseph	Mrs. Claus	Ornaments	Christmas Cards	Santa's List
Star	Sleigh	Cookies and Milk	Mittens	Ho! Ho! Ho!
Toys	Rudolph	Carolers	Sled	Gold, Frankincense, and Myrrh

ANGEL

A	N	G	E	L
Baby Jesus, Mary and Joseph	Mrs. Claus	Ornaments	Christmas Cards	Santa's List
Star	Sleigh	Cookies and Milk	Mittens	Ho! Ho! Ho!
Toys	Rudolph	Carolers	Sled	Gold, Frankincense, and Myrrh
Santa Claus	December 25th	Christmas Mouse	Candle	Bethlehem
Three Wise Men	Candy Cane	Chimney	Noel	Poinsettia

A	N	G	E	L
Toys	Rudolph	Carolers	Sled	Gold, Frankincense, and Myrrh
Santa Claus	December 25th	Christmas Mouse	Candle	Bethlehem
Three Wise Men	Candy Cane	Chimney	Noel	Poinsettia
North Pole	Presents	Stocking	Christmas Lights	Hot Cocoa
Ebenezer Scrooge	Snowman	Wreath	Silent Night	Holly and Berries

A	N	G	E	L
Three Wise Men	Candy Cane	Chimney	Noel	Poinsettia
North Pole	Presents	Stocking	Christmas Lights	Hot Cocoa
Ebenezer Scrooge	Snowman	Wreath	Silent Night	Holly and Berries
Snowflake	Christmas Tree	Praying Hands	Drummer Boy	Letters to Santa
Angel	Elf	Jingle Bells	Happy New Year	Gingerbread Men

A	N	G	E	L
Angel	Presents	Stocking	Christmas Lights	Gingerbread Men
Santa Claus	Mrs. Claus	Praying Hands	Silent Night	Poinsettia
Star	Elf	Cookies and Milk	Candle	Bethlehem
Baby Jesus, Mary and Joseph	Rudolph	Carolers	Mittens	Santa's List
Ebenezer Scrooge	Christmas Tree	Ornaments	Christmas Cards	Hot Cocoa

A — Baby Jesus, Mary and Joseph

E — Christmas Cards

A — Santa Claus

N — Elf

A — Angel

G — Praying Hands

N — Mrs. Claus

L — Poinsettia

N — Rudolph

L — Gold, Frankincense, and Myrrh

L — Bethlehem

A — Ebenezer Scrooge

N — Sleigh

E — Drummer Boy

G — Carolers

A — Three Wise Men

E — Candle

L — Hot Cocoa

E — Silent Night

E — Happy New Year

A — Star

E — Christmas Lights

L — Santa's List

N — Presents

G — Stocking

N Snowman	**N** Christmas Tree	**L** Holly and Berries	**L** Letters to Santa	**N** Candy Cane
G Ornaments	**E** Mittens	**G** Wreath	**E** Noel	**L** Ho! Ho! Ho!
G Chimney	**L** Gingerbread Men	**A** North Pole	**G** Christmas Mouse	**G** Cookies and Milk
E Sled	**N** December 25th	**A** Snowflake	**G** Jingle Bells	**A** Toys

Secret Christmas Angel

Supplies

Pencil

Purple construction paper

White construction paper

Scissors

Yellow construction paper

Stapler

Crayons

Tacky glue

Paper hole puncher

Paper fastener

Silver glitter

White note card

Red pen

Directions

1. Trace the following pattern pieces onto the construction paper and cut out: two purple wings (pattern piece #1), one white face (pattern piece #2), and one purple halo (pattern piece #3).

2. Bend the yellow construction paper into a cone shape to form an angel's body. Trim the bottom and staple closed. Cut a pocket from extra construction paper and glue it onto the front of the angel.

3. Draw an angel's face onto the face with the crayons.

4. Glue the face to the neck of the body.

5. Glue the halo to the back of the head.

6. Punch a hole in the angel's back and the center of each wing at the straight edge. Then poke the paper fastener through both wings and the angel's back. Close the paper fastener and keep the wings down so they stay hidden behind the body.

7. Glue glitter onto the halo, wings, and body.

8. On a note card write the following verse and instructions:

    I'm a Secret Christmas Angel,

    Trying to earn my wings.

    If you do a good deed on earth,

    All of heaven sings!

    Slide my wings out from behind me, but please do a good deed first!

    Then sign it, "from your Secret Christmas Pal." Slide it into the pocket.

9. Deliver the angel to someone's front door, ring the doorbell, and run!

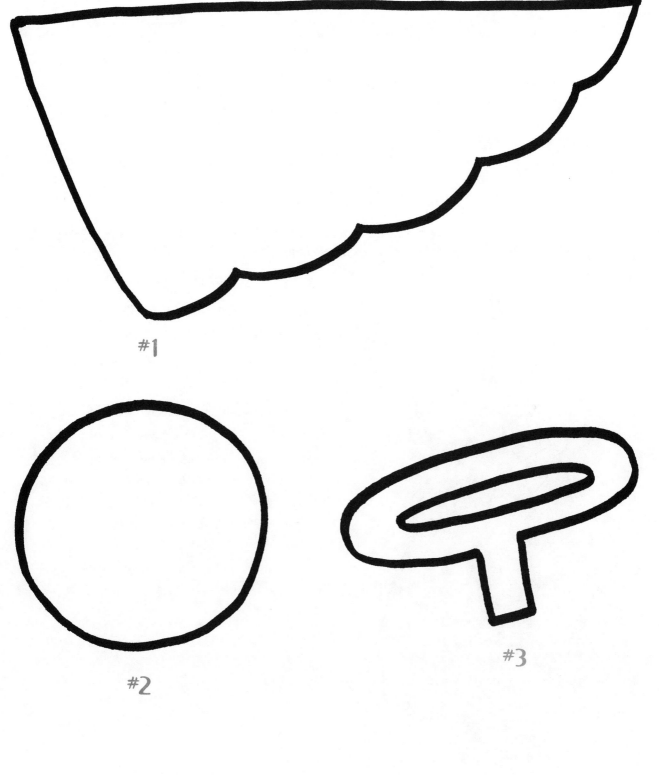

#1

#2

#3

Earn Your Wings

Supplies

Pencil

Purple construction paper

White construction paper

Scissors

Yellow construction paper

Stapler

String

Jingle bell

Tacky glue or glue gun

Feathers (assorted colors, found at craft stores)

Christmas tree

Directions

1. Trace the following pattern pieces found on page 63 onto construction paper and cut out: two purple wings per player (pattern piece #1), one white face (pattern piece #2), and one purple halo (pattern piece #3).

2. Bend the yellow construction paper into a cone shape to form an angel's body. Trim the bottom and staple closed.

3. Draw an angel's face onto the face with the crayons.

4. Glue the face to the neck of the body.

5. Glue the halo to the back of the head.

6. Attach string to the bell and tie it around the angel's neck.

7. Have everyone glue feathers to their wings. Let the wings dry a little before playing the game.

8. To play the game, place the angel on top of the Christmas tree. Let each child take a turn tossing his wings at the tree hoping to reach the angel. If his wings hit the angel hard enough, the bell will ring and the angel will earn its wings

Note: If you use a glue gun, the glue dries instantly and you can start the game.

Be an Angel, Don't Make a Mess

Supplies

Two 6-ounce packages lime gelatin

Two 6-ounce packages cherry gelatin

Measuring cup

Large saucepan

Water

Two large bowls

Two large spoons

Two large bowls

Fifty marbles

Newspaper

Paper towels

Optional: Two chairs

Directions

1. Make the lime and cherry gelatin according to the package directions in different bowls. Refrigerate.

2. Break up the gelatin with the spoons, then add twenty-five marbles to each bowl. Stir to mix the marbles and gelatin together.

3. Play this game in the kitchen, near a sink, or outside (if it's warm) near a hose.

4. Divide the players into two teams: the green and the red teams.

5. Set a bowl of the lime (green) gelatin in front of one team, and the bowl of cherry (red) gelatin in front of the other team.

6. Lay newspaper on each side of the bowls.

7. The object of the game is to put your foot into the bowl of gelatin, find the marbles, collect them with your toes, and put them on the newspaper. Have a timed race between teams. A few rules apply: toes only allowed, change players within your team anytime (the gelatin gets cold), gelatin stays in the bowl—Be an Angel, Don't Make a Mess.

8. The winning team is the one who collects the most marbles after 10 minutes with the least amount of gelatin on its newspaper, and the least amount of additional mess. Have an adult be the judge.

9. Decide if players can wipe their feet off after their turn or need to wait until the game is over. Have lots of paper towels.

Optional: Give each team a chair that the player can sit on.

The Perfect Snow Angel

Two children dressed
  for snow
Fresh fallen snow

Angel Pick-up Sticks

Fifty pieces angel
  hair pasta
Wax paper
Red spray paint
Green spray paint

Angel Bingo

White copy paper
Scissors
Mini marshmallows
Bell
Tape
Optional: Garland
  and glue
Variation: Crayons

Secret Christmas Angel

Pencil
Purple construction
  paper
White construction
  paper
Scissors
Yellow construction
  paper
Stapler
Crayons
Tacky glue
Paper hole puncher
Paper fastener
Silver glitter
White note card
Red pen

Earn Your Wings

Pencil
Purple construction
  paper
White construction
  paper
Scissors
Yellow construction
  paper
Stapler
String
Jingle bell
Tacky glue or glue gun
Feathers (assorted
  colors, found at
  craft stores)
Christmas tree

Supplies for I Believe in Angels

Be an Angel, Don't Make a Mess

Two 6-ounce packages
  lime gelatin
Two 6-ounce packages
  cherry gelatin
Measuring cup
Large saucepan
Water
Two large bowls
Two large spoons
Two large bowls
Fifty marbles
Newspaper
Paper towels
Optional: Two chairs

Don't forget the
camera and film

Christmas Tree in the Making

Japan

Supplies		
	Construction paper	Glue
	Scissors	Tape
Crayons or markers	Green plastic trash bags	

Directions

1. Divide the players into groups of four to six. You will want several different teams, so adjust the groups accordingly. Choose one player on each team to be the "Christmas Tree." The others will be "decorators."

2. First, they can all draw Christmas tree decorations on construction paper and cut them out.

3. Have the "decorators" wrap their "Christmas Trees" with the green plastic trash bags, staying below their trees' necks, of course.

4. They can then glue or tape their teams' decorations to their trees.

5. After all the Christmas trees have been decorated, take a vote from all the players to decide which tree is the best.

What is the best Christmas gift you received as an adult?

"One of my friends, whose major is music therapy, sends me a cassette tape every Christmas. He and I played the piano together, and often listened to music all night long. His cassette tapes are filled with gentle music of good memories."
—Masako Matumoto
Mizuho, Nagoya
Japan

Christmas Here, There, and Everywhere — Global Celebrations

Lola and Her Coins
Philippines

Supplies

A grandmother (or child/adult dressed like a grandmother)

Chair

Lots of chocolate coins

Directions

1. Have the grandmother (Lola) sit in a chair.

2. Each child comes before her and performs by singing a Christmas song, telling a Christmas story, or making up a Christmas poem.

3. Lola gives the performing child one to ten chocolate coins, depending on how well he did. He can get back in line to perform again.

A highlight at Christmastime in the Philippines is Lola, the beloved grandmother always remembered for the many games she played with children.

Unscramble Eskimo Christmas Food
Alaska

Supplies

White paper

Red and green crayons, colored pencils, or markers (one per player)

Seven wrapped prizes (try to find prizes to go with each food scrambled—for example, a stuffed polar bear or a whale key chain

Directions

1. Make copies of the whale puzzle on the following page, one per player.

2. Each player gets a crayon, pencil, or marker, and a whale puzzle.

3. The first person to get all the words (Eskimo foods) unscrambled correctly chooses a prize. Then the second person to do the same chooses a prize and so on until all seven prizes have been won.

4. Here are the answers:

   1. Beluga Whale   5. Eider Duck
   2. Caribou   6. Maktak
   3. Seal   7. Ptarmigan
   4. Walrus

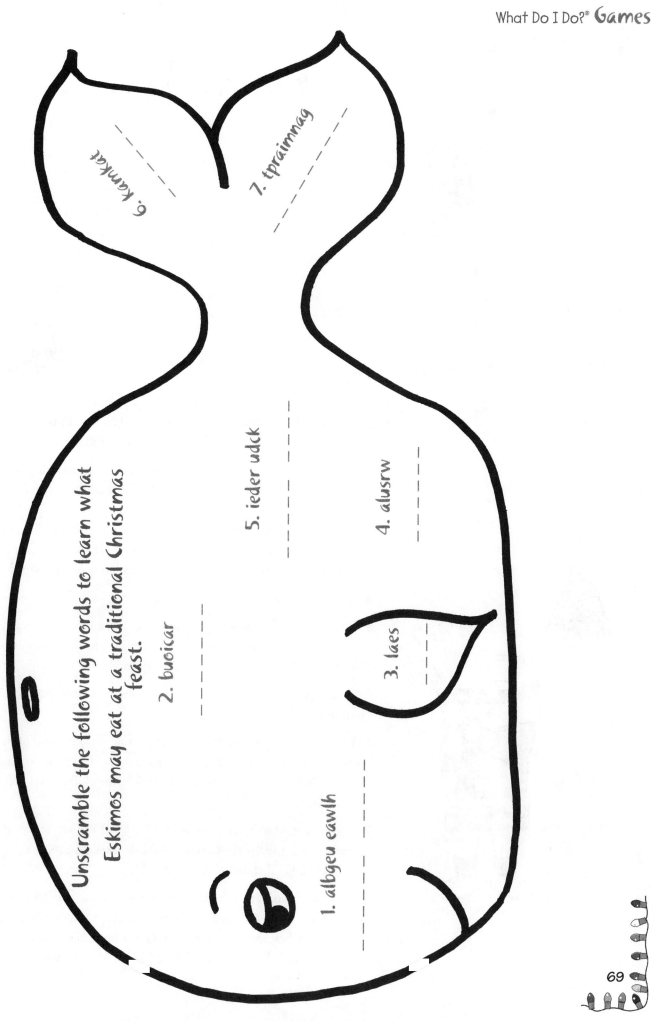

Unscramble the following words to learn what Eskimos may eat at a traditional Christmas feast.

6. kamkat

7. tpraimnay

5. ieder udck

4. alusrw

2. buoicar

3. laes

1. albgeu eawlh

69

Piñata Fun
Mexico

1 – uno
2 – dos
3 – tres
4 – cuatro
5 – cinco
6 – seis
7 – siete
8 – ocho
9 – nueve
10 – diez
11 – once
12 – doce
13 – trece
14 – catorce
15 – quince

Supplies

Scissors

Paper

Red permanent marker

Stapler

Christmas wrapping paper

Tape

Christmas prizes

Christmas piñata (purchased or homemade)

Christmas candy

Small Christmas trinkets

Rope

Blindfold

Large stick

Optional: Two piñatas, or extra prizes, and a basket of extra trinkets and candy

Directions

1. Before the party, decide how many prizes you would like to give away; this doesn't include the trinkets needed for the piñatas. Then cut the paper into 2-inch squares (one for each prize). Fold each square in half.

2. On each square, write one Spanish number on the outside and the corresponding English number on the inside. Start with number "one" (*uno*) and continue in order. (English numbers and their Spanish equivalents through "fifteen" (*quince*) are in the sidebar of this page.) Play with any amount of numbers you choose. If you go over fifteen you will need to find out how to write those numbers in Spanish.

3. Staple each square closed.

4. Wrap all the Christmas prizes, then write a Spanish number on each starting with uno and continuing in order. Put the prizes under a Christmas tree or other area near the piñata.

5. Fill the piñata with candy, trinkets, and the numbered papers you stapled closed.

6. Tie one end of the rope to the piñata; throw the other end of the rope over a tree branch (or something similar). The piñata will need to be pulled up and down by an adult while the children are taking turns hitting it.

7. Choose a child to break the piñata for the first round. At birthday parties, this is usually the birthday child. So perhaps choose the child's whose birthday is closest to December 25.

8. First, blindfold him, then give him the large stick, twirl him around a few times, and let him take three whacks at the piñata. Others can yell out the piñata's whereabouts. If the child doesn't break the piñata, give another child a chance. Always blindfold the players and spin them around first.

9. Once the piñata breaks, all the kids scramble to retrieve as much of the candy, trinkets, and numbered pieces of paper as possible.

10. Once they realize they have collected numbers, take them to the Christmas prizes. Ask who has *uno* (one). That child should come up and find a Christmas prize marked *uno* and so on. (If the children can't understand the Spanish words, they can open their papers to see the English translation.)

11. You must decide ahead of time whether or not you want the kids to open their prizes immediately after getting them, or waiting until all numbers have been turned in.

Optional: Some kids will not get as many goodies as others, so you may want to have a second piñata for a second round, or extra prizes, trinkets, and candy.

Tip: Let as many kids as possible take turns at trying to break the piñata—perhaps limit the swings to one per person. All kids want to be the piñata breaker.

The piñata originated in Italy. Called *pignatta*, it meant "fragile pot."

Amigo Secrets
Brazil

Supplies	Paper	Pens	Bowl

Directions

1. This game is usually played with family members, co-workers, or school children. Have everyone put his or her name on a piece of paper then into the bowl.

2. Everyone draws a slip of paper out of the bowl, revealing a name that they keep a secret. They will then buy that person a present to exchange later.

3. In Brazil, the presents are usually gag gifts, so there are lots of laughs when it's time to do the exchange.

In Brazil, there is a law called the "13th salary" that makes sure all workers will be able to afford Christmas. Workers receive an extra month's salary, sometimes split between November and December's paychecks, also called a "Christmas bonus."

Guess Who the Mummers Are?
Canada

During the twelve days of Christmas, people would disguise themselves with all sorts of clothing, then go to different houses and ask, "any mummers allowed in?" They would entertain by telling jokes, dancing, and singing, and let people guess who they were. The mummers would be served a Christmas drink and dessert before going on to the next house.

Supplies

		Sweaters	Make-up
		Lace	Coats
Scarves	Boots	Fabric	Pillows
Masks	Socks	Long dresses	Nightgowns
Pillowcases	Long underwear	Pantyhose	Towels
Hats	Sheets	Blankets	Goggles

Directions

1. This game is a take off of "mummering," a very popular tradition in Newfoundland, Canada, a long time ago. See the educational fact in the sidebar to learn more about mummering.

2. Divide the players into two groups.

3. Take one group out of the room where all the supply items have been laid out on the floor. Include any other items you think would work well.

4. Let them use any of the items to disguise themselves completely from head to toe. Give them about 15 minutes to do so.

5. While the first group is dressing, let the second group enjoy a Christmas snack and drink. Instruct them to answer "yes" when the first group asks them a question.

6. Explain to the dressed group that they will go in front of the other group and perform. When they enter the room they should ask, "Any mummers allowed in?" They then sing, dance, tell jokes, or whatever, one at a time, while the other group guesses who they are. Set a time limit according to your schedule.

7. When everyone in the first group has performed, give them Christmas snacks and drinks while the others disguise themselves.

Supplies for Christmas Here, There, and Everywhere—Global Celebrations

Christmas Tree in the Making
Japan

Crayons or markers
Construction paper
Scissors
Green plastic trash bags
Glue
Tape

Lola and Her Coins
Philippines

A grandmother (or child/adult dressed like a grandmother)
Chair
Lots of chocolate coins

Unscramble Eskimo Christmas Food
Alaska

White paper
Red and green crayons, colored pencils, or markers (one per player)
Seven wrapped prizes (try to find prizes to go with each food scrambled—for example, a stuffed polar bear or a whale key chain

Piñata Fun
Mexico

Scissors
Paper
Red permanent marker
Stapler
Christmas wrapping paper
Tape
Christmas prizes

(continued)

Christmas piñata (purchased or home-made)
Christmas candy
Small Christmas trinkets
Rope
Blindfold
Large stick
Optional: Two piñatas, or extra prizes, and a basket of extra trinkets and candy

Amigo Secrets
Brazil

Paper
Pens
Bowl

Don't forget the camera and film

Guess Who the Mummers Are?
Canada

Scarves
Masks
Pillowcases
Hats
Boots
Socks
Long underwear
Sheets
Sweaters
Lace
Fabric
Long dresses
Pantyhose
Blankets
Make-up
Coats
Pillows
Nightgowns
Towels
Goggles

CHAPTER 3
Crafts and Favors

Helpful Hints for Crafts and Favors

1. Be prepared with all supplies and directions.

2. When supplies are limited, remind everyone it's important to take turns and share.

3. Have a finished example of the craft to show everyone.

4. If an item is listed in the supply list without a quantity, you need only one.

5. Most ideas in this chapter make one craft.

6. Allow approximately 15 to 30 minutes to do most of the crafts.

7. Many of the crafts would make excellent gifts, especially for those you need to give something little to, but want that homemade touch.

8. Some of the favors in this chapter incorporate food which can be used for the party.

9. Some of the craft ideas in this section can be used in place of a game.

10. If the craft needs time to dry, make it at the beginning of the party.

11. Be sure to label each craft with its owner's name. One way is to label paper plates and lay the crafts on them.

12. Put your name and date somewhere on the crafts you keep or give each year. It's fun to see when you or your children made them, especially since it stops any argument about which child made what when.

13. Keep in mind, people have different levels of ability. One might hurry through a craft while another might need more time to complete it.

14. Younger children comprehend directions better before they begin on their craft, but they use their imagination to create, so don't overwhelm them with directions.

15. Try to have one adult helper for every four young children.

16. Always have adult supervision when using glue guns, X-acto® knives, or other sharp or potentially dangerous tools.

17. A glue gun will save you a lot of time, but children may be safer using school or tacky glue.

18. Use safety scissors with a rounded tip for very young children, or cut out items before the party.

19. When cutting felt or fabric, use a sharp pair of scissors made for fabric.

20. Younger children do better with simpler crafts while older children can handle longer directions, more decision making, and more supplies.

21. Ask older children the following when they're making their craft:
    - Can you take away something, add something? What?
    - Can it be smaller, taller, fatter, thinner, or a different color?

22. Praise children when they are done with their craft.

23. When making crafts at home with your children, have them help with clean-up. When making crafts at a party, however, you may want to leave the mess until your guests have gone.

24. Use newspaper, wax paper, or butcher paper under your work area to help with clean-up. When you're done crafting, just fold up the paper and throw it away.

25. Lay wax paper under your project when painting. If you don't have any try putting clear packaging tape over any paper. It works just as well.

26. Always let paint dry thoroughly before adding another coat. Play games or have refreshments in-between coats.

27. Save lids from jars for glue, beads, or paint. Pour small amounts into the lids, one per child or small group.

28. The glue in glue sticks comes in different colors, so be careful to choose colors that blend and won't show through.

29. A toothpick, instead of a pencil, works well to trace onto craft foam.

30. When using reusable adhesive, roll it in your hand to soften it first.

31. When a craft project calls for a star, use a star eraser.

32. A pipe cleaner is also called a chenille stem.

33. A paper fastener is also called a brad.

34. Poster board is also called tag board.

35. Several craft projects in this chapter call for beads; they may be called different names depending on the brand and store you buy them at. If you can, take the illustration with you when you shop.

36. Moving eyes are sometimes called "wiggly" or "googly" eyes.

37. A craft stick is also a Popsicle® stick.

38. Take pictures and/or videos so you'll have lasting memories.

39. Listen to Christmas music while making crafts.

40. Watch for 50% off coupons and other great deals at craft stores for supplies. Don't forget the after-Christmas sales!

Jumbo Popcorn Stocking

Perfect for a Secret Santa gift. Add a six-pack of pop and you've got a winner—a definite Wow!

Supplies

Jumbo see-through plastic stocking

Popcorn

Version 1: Stocking with snap-close handle

Version 2: Stapler, glue, and Christmas ribbon

Version 3: Ribbon or raffia

Directions

Pop lots and lots of popcorn and fill the stocking full. Follow one of the versions below to close the stocking:

Version 1: Purchase stocking with a snap-close handle.

Version 2: Staple the top of the stocking shut, then glue Christmas ribbon around the stapled edge.

Version 3: Gather the top of the stocking and tie with ribbon or raffia.

Note: Oriental Trading® Company Inc. sells a 27½-inch plastic holiday stocking with a handle. For availability and pricing call 1-800-246-8400, or write them at P.O. Box 3407, Omaha, Nebraska 68103, or go to www.oriental.com.

Painted Swirled Ornaments

Supplies

Clear round ornaments

Acrylic paints (assorted colors)

Paper towels

Variation: Tinsel, paintbrushes

Directions

1. Carefully pull the hook off an ornament.

2. Squirt one color of paint inside the ornament and swirl it around.

3. Repeat step #2 as many times as you want with different colors.

4. Turn the ornament upside down on a paper towel overnight to dry, then replace the hook.

5. Repeat steps #1 through #4 for the other ornaments.

Variation: Fill the ornament with tinsel, and paint your name and a design on the outside.

Legend of the Candy Cane

Supplies

Computer

Red card stock

Scissors

Paper hole puncher

2 feet ¼" green ribbon

Candy cane with one large and three small red stripes

Glue gun

Optional: Small plastic sprig holly and berries

Directions

1. Research the legend of the candy cane on the Internet or at the library. There are several versions. Choose one that appeals to you and type it in a 3 x 3-inch textbox and print it on the red card stock.

2. Cut out the textbox and punch a hole in the top left corner.

3. Cut the ribbon in half and tie one piece around the center of the candy cane and through the hole in the card stock before tying it into a bow.

4. Make a bow from the other half and glue it on top of the first bow. Trim excess ribbon if needed.

Optional: Glue the holly and berries on top of the bows.

Paperback Christmas Tree

Supplies

Old paperback book

Stapler

Green spray paint

Optional: Glitter

Directions

1. Fold the top right corner of a page down to the center of the page, then fold the bottom right corner up to meet the top half, and to form a point at the side of the page.

2. Repeat step #1 for all the pages and both the back and front covers, folding all pages in the same direction.

3. Bend back the covers to fan out the book, and staple together along with more pages if needed to keep the "tree" evenly spread out.

4. Spray paint the entire tree and let dry.

Optional: Immediately sprinkle glitter on the tree after painting.

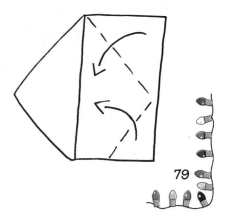

Christmas Tree Foam Puzzle

In the 1800's, German settlers were the first to use Christmas trees in the United States.

Can you give us some ideas on how to decorate the outside of a house?

"In Chicago, Marshall Field's department store has been famous since the 1890's for its elaborate holiday window displays. But in recent years, homeowners throughout Chicago and its suburbs have been creating some pretty spectacular displays of their own. The latest trend is to lift the garage door, cover the opening with sheets of clear acrylic, and fill the garage with a three-dimensional holiday display. Local creative decorators have treated thousands of onlookers to such delights as a snowy amusement park, a five-level train village, and a life-size stable for Santa's reindeer. Of course, their cars are left in the cold, unless they're as crafty as one homeowner who displayed Santa in the garage riding his shiny red Corvette!"

—Mary Edsey
Author of The Best Christmas Decorations in Chicagoland

Supplies

9 x 12-inch green craft foam

Ruler

Red permanent marker

Pencil

X-acto® knife

Cutting board at least 9 x 12 inches (cardboard will work)

Directions

1. Fold the craft foam in half lengthwise and in thirds widthwise, then unfold it to reveal six 4½ x 4-inch squares. Draw lines on the crease marks with the ruler and red permanent marker.

2. Use the pencil to trace Christmas trees (pattern pieces #1 through #6) onto the green craft foam, one tree in each square.

3. Lay the craft foam onto the cutting board. Using the X-acto® knife, carefully cut out the Christmas trees, keeping each in one piece without cutting any other part of the foam.

4. You now have a puzzle for young children. Take out the trees, mix them up, and have kids put them back into the correct shapes.

#1

#2

#3

#4

#5

#6

Christmas Tree Journal or Centerpiece

Supplies

8½ x 11-inch green card stock (65 lb.) (two pieces for centerpiece)

Three pieces 8½ x 11-inch white computer paper (none for centerpiece)

Pencil

Scissors

Stapler

Optional: Markers, glitter, beads/jewels, glue, and paints/paintbrushes

Directions for Journal

1. Fold the cardstock and white computer paper in half widthwise. Keep all the white computer paper folded together.

2. Trace the outer Christmas tree (pattern piece #1) onto the green folded card stock with the straight edge at the fold, then cut out.

3. Trace the inner Christmas tree (pattern piece #2) onto the white computer paper with the straight edge at the fold, then cut through all the layers.

4. Slide the white trees into the green tree.

5. Open up the journal; you should have a green border all around the white tree. Adjust the white paper if needed. Staple all the sheets together at the fold, once at the top and once at the bottom of the tree. Close your journal.

Optional: Decorate the front of your journal using any or all of the following: markers, glitter, beads/jewels, glue, and paints/paintbrushes.

Directions for Centerpiece

1. Lay both pieces of green card stock on top of each other and fold the paper in half lengthwise.

2. Freehand, cut out half a Christmas tree with the tip at one end of the fold and the trunk at the other.

3. Open up the cardstock and place two staples in the fold, both near the center of the tree.

4. Fan out the cardstock for a four-sided tree and stand it on a table for a centerpiece.

Optional: Decorate your centerpiece using any or all of the following: markers, glitter, beads/jewels, glue, and paints/paintbrushes.

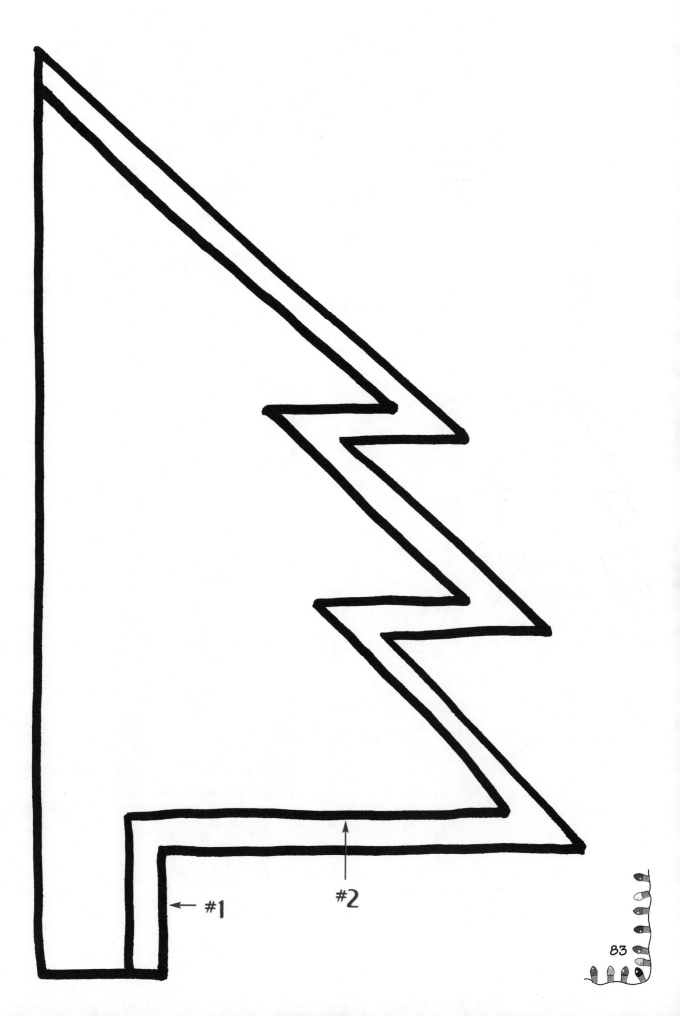

#1

#2

Supplies for Christmas Trees, Stockings, and Candy Canes

Jumbo Popcorn Stocking

Jumbo see-through
  plastic stocking
Popcorn
Version 1:
  Stocking with
  snap-close handle
Version 2:
  Stapler, glue, and
  Christmas ribbon
Version 3:
  Ribbon or raffia

Painted Swirled Ornaments

Clear round
  ornaments
Acrylic paints
  (assorted colors)
Paper towels
Variation: Tinsel,
  paintbrushes

Legend of the Candy Cane

Computer
Red card stock
Scissors
Paper hole puncher
2 feet ¼" green ribbon
Candy cane with one
  large and three
  small red stripes
Glue gun
Optional: Small plastic
  sprig holly and berries

Paperback Christmas Tree

Old paperback book
Stapler
Green spray paint
Optional: Glitter

Christmas Tree Foam Puzzle

9 x 12-inch green
  craft foam
Ruler
Red permanent marker
Pencil
X-acto® knife
Cutting board at
  least 9 x 12 inches
  (cardboard will work)

Christmas Tree Journal or Centerpiece

8½ x 11-inch green
  card stock (65 lb.)
  (two pieces for
  centerpiece)
Three pieces
  8½ x 11-inch white
  computer paper
  (none for centerpiece)
Pencil
Scissors
Stapler
Optional: Markers,
  glitter, beads/jewels,
  glue, and paints/
  paintbrushes

Don't forget the
camera and film

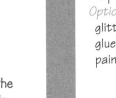

Toilet Paper Snowman

Supplies

Man's white tube sock

Roll of toilet paper

4-inch Styrofoam® ball

Twist tie

Scissors

Fabric (any color)

Glue gun

Four 1-inch black pom-poms

Two moving eyes

Orange pipe cleaner

Five 5mm black pom-poms

For a boy snowman, add a 5-inch snowman hat (found at craft stores)

For a girl snowman, add fake eyelashes, a large plastic sprig holly and berries, and a 5-inch doll hat (all found at craft stores)

Directions

1. Turn the sock inside out (for a fluffier snowman) and stuff the roll of toilet paper into the toe portion. Hide any excess toe up inside the toilet paper roll.

2. Push the Styrofoam® ball into the sock to sit on top of the toilet paper. Stretch the sock if needed.

3. Gather the excess sock above the ball and use the twist tie to secure it tightly.

4. Cut a ½-inch piece of fabric 18 inches long. Tie it around the snowman's neck for a scarf, between the toilet paper and Styrofoam® ball.

5. Glue the four large black pom-poms down from the scarf for buttons.

6. Glue the moving eyes to the snowman's face.

7. Cut a 1-inch piece of pipe cleaner and glue it to the face, pointing straight out, for a carrot nose.

8. Glue the five small pom-poms in a curved shape just under the nose for the mouth.

9. Glue either the snowman or doll hat on top of the snowman.

10. For a girl snowman, cut, fit, and glue the eyelashes above the eyes, and glue the holly and berries to the scarf area.

Snow, Snowmen, and Snowflakes

Frosty the Snowman Sock

Supplies

White crew sock

Polyester stuffing

Tacky glue

12 inches white ribbon

Scissors

3-inch square black felt

1 x 18-inch Christmas fabric

Two ¼-inch black pom-poms

Orange permanent marker

Five 7mm black pom-poms

Three 1-inch black pom-poms

Directions

1. Fill the sock with stuffing.

2. Loop and glue the ribbon to the inside of the sock for a hanger. Then glue the sock opening closed.

3. Cut a snowman's hat from the black felt, big enough to cover the ankle portion of the sock. Glue it to the ankle so the snowman will be standing up when held by the handle.

4. Tie the strip of fabric (scarf) around the snowman's "neck," a couple of inches down from the hat.

5. Glue the two ¼-inch black pom-poms right below the hat for eyes.

6. Draw a nose on the snowman's face with the orange permanent marker.

7. Glue the five 7mm black pom-poms under the nose for a mouth, leaving a little space between them.

8. Glue the three 1-inch black pom-poms down from the scarf for the buttons.

You are the Snowman

uring winter
Search the
for snow sculp-
ou'll be amazed at
ou find, and may
ecide you can do
ht in your own
rd.

Supplies

Pencil

Cardboard

Scissors

Tacky glue

Cotton balls

Picture of yourself
(head shot)

Toothpicks

Three ½-inch black
pom-poms

Picture hanger
(self-adhesive)

Option 1: 6 inches
½" ribbon

Option 2: Black felt

Directions

1. Trace the following pattern pieces onto the cardboard and cut out: one snowman head (pattern piece #1), one snowman middle (pattern piece #2), and one snowman bottom (pattern piece #3).

2. Slightly overlapping the three circles, glue them together to make a snowman.

3. Glue cotton balls onto the two larger circles (the snowman's body).

4. Glue your picture onto the smallest circle (the snowman's head) then trim to fit.

5. Glue small pieces of cotton around your picture.

6. Glue toothpicks to the center circle, one on each side for arms.

7. Glue the black pom-poms on the snowman's body for buttons.

8. Attach the picture hanger to the back.

Option 1: If you would prefer loop and glue the ribbon to the back of the head for a hanger.

Option 2: Cut a snowman hat from black felt and glue on head.

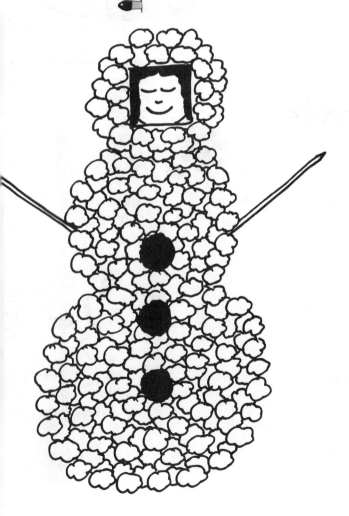

Magical Snow Globe

Supplies

Empty baby food jar

Glue gun

Small plastic
Christmas figurine

Glycerin (found at
drug stores)

Water

White glitter

Optional:
Silicone glue

Directions

1. Wash and dry the baby food jar.

2. Glue the Christmas figurine to the inside of the jar lid.

3. Fill the jar almost to the top with half glycerin and half water.

4. Sprinkle glitter on top of the water mixture.

5. Screw the lid on the jar, making sure it's tight. Then glue around
   the outside edge of the lid.

6. Shake the globe to mix the glycerin and water, then shake to
   watch the falling snow.

Optional: Use silicone glue around the outside edge of the lid.

Snow Paints

Supplies

Four spray bottles

Food coloring (red,
blue, yellow, green)

Fresh fallen snow

Optional: Squirt bottles

Directions

1. Fill the spray bottles with water.

2. One color per bottle, add food coloring several drops at a time and shake
   to mix. Continue adding more until you get your desired color.

3. Spray designs onto fresh fallen snow or on things you make from snow such
   as snowmen or igloos.

Optional: Squirt bottles can be used along with, or in place of, spray bottles.

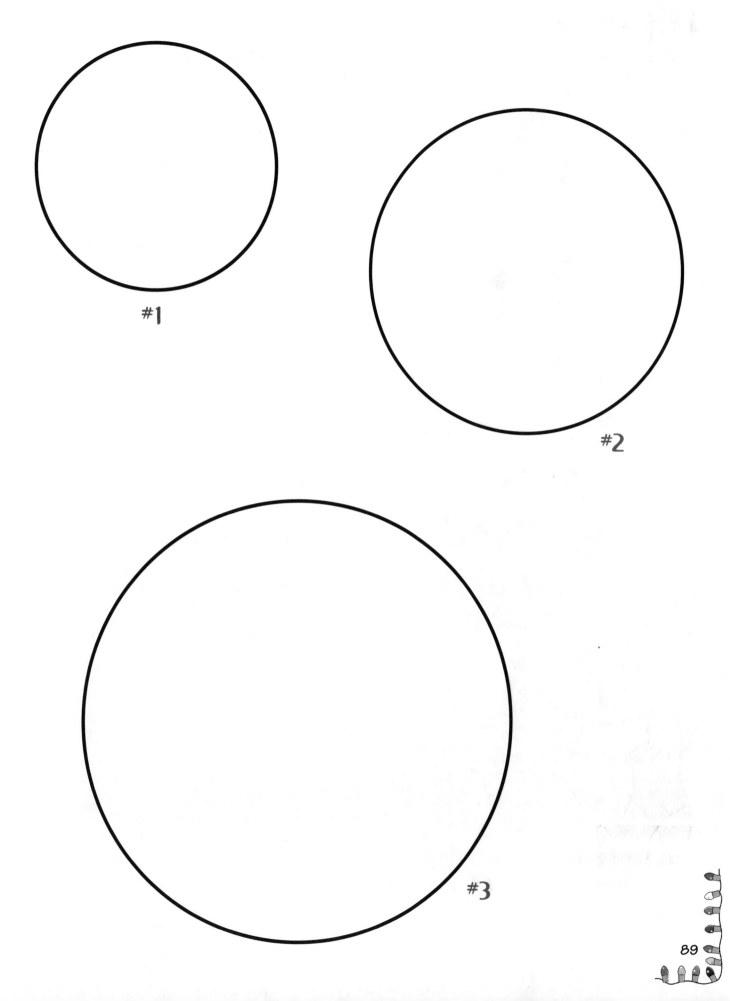

#1

#2

#3

Doily Snowman

Supplies

5-inch white doily

6-inch white doily

8-inch white doily

Glue stick

Two 16mm moving eyes

Toothpick

Paintbrush

Orange acrylic paint

Five 7mm black pom-poms

Three ¾-inch black pom-poms

Scissors

Black construction paper

2 inches magnetic tape

Directions

1. Slightly overlap the three doilies, smallest on top and largest on bottom in a snowman pattern. Glue in place.

2. Glue the moving eyes to the 5-inch doily (head).

3. Break the toothpick in half.

4. Glue one of the toothpick halves (at the broken end) to the snowman under the eyes for a carrot nose.

5. Paint the toothpick (nose) orange.

6. Glue the five 7mm black pom-poms under the nose to form a mouth.

7. Glue the three ¾-inch black pom-poms to the 6-inch doily (snowman's body) for buttons.

8. Cut a snowman's hat from the black construction paper and glue to the top of the snowman's head.

9. Secure magnetic tape to the back of the snowman and put it on your refrigerator.

Toilet Paper Snowman

Man's white tube sock
Roll of toilet paper
4-inch Styrofoam® ball
Twist tie
Scissors
Fabric (any color)
Glue gun
Four 1-inch black
  pom-poms
Two moving eyes
Orange pipe cleaner
Five 5mm black
  pom-poms
For a boy snowman,
  add a 5-inch
  snowman hat (found
  at craft stores)
For a girl snowman,
  add fake eyelashes,
  a large plastic sprig
  holly and berries, and
  a 5-inch doll hat
  (all found at craft
  stores)

Don't forget the
camera and film

Frosty the Snowman Sock

White crew sock
Polyester stuffing
Tacky glue
12 inches white ribbon
Scissors
3-inch square
  black felt
1 x 18-inch Christmas
  fabric
Two ¼-inch black
  pom-poms
Orange permanent
  marker
Five 7mm black
  pom-poms
Three 1-inch black
  pom-poms

Magical Snow Globe

Empty baby food jar
Glue gun
Small plastic
  Christmas figurine
Glycerin (found at
  drug stores)
Water
White glitter
Optional: Silicone glue

Supplies for Snow, Snowmen, and Snowflakes

Snow Paints

Four spray bottles
Food coloring (red,
  blue, yellow, green)
Fresh fallen snow
Optional: Squirt bottles

You are the Snowman

Pencil
Cardboard
Scissors
Tacky glue
Cotton balls
Picture of yourself
  (head shot)
Toothpicks
Three ½-inch black
  pom-poms
Picture hanger
  (self-adhesive)
Option 1: 6 inches
⅛" ribbon
Option 2: Black felt

Doily Snowman

5-inch white doily
6-inch white doily
8-inch white doily
Glue stick
Two 16mm moving eyes
Toothpick
Paintbrush
Orange acrylic paint
Five 7mm black
  pom-poms
Three ¾-inch black
  pom-poms
Scissors
Black construction
  paper
2 inches magnetic tape

A Gift from Santa

What is the best Christmas gift you received as an adult? "My mom and dad gave me a very elegant coupon book they made. Each coupon showed a photograph of them doing what the coupon offered. For example the one for babysitting showed my mom with my children. Another special coupon was an offer of decorated cakes for any party or shower I wanted to give; the photo showed my mother with a tray of individual baby bootie cakes. Also, there was a photo of my mom holding one my favorite dishes. My dad had a coupon for a family portrait done in sepia-tone. The coupon book was put together in a beautiful, thoughtful, and loving way, and it was funny and personal to our family."

—Nancy Savage
Author of Nickel The Baby Buffalo Who Thought He Was A Dog
Golden, Colorado

Supplies

Small rectangular box with gift inside

Red wrapping paper

Scissors

Tape

Yellow construction paper

Wide black ribbon

Black permanent marker

Directions

1. Wrap the box with a gift inside with the red paper. Tape to secure.

2. Cut out a rectangle from the yellow construction paper, the size of a large belt buckle. Then cut out a small rectangle from the middle of the belt buckle, leaving a vertical strip in the center so you can weave a ribbon through the buckle.

3. Weave the black ribbon through the belt buckle.

4. Wrap the "belt buckle ribbon," lengthwise, around the present. Tape to secure.

5. Use the black permanent marker to write the following below the belt buckle, substituting the recipient's name:
   To Donna, Merry Christmas, Ho! Ho! Ho!

Elf Handprints

Supplies

Pencil

Twenty-six sheets green construction paper

Scissors

Cardboard

Tacky glue

Red construction paper

Green and red glitter

Picture hanger (self-adhesive)

Directions

1. Trace one hand onto the twenty-six sheets of green construction paper. You may not need as much paper for smaller hands.

2. Cut the hand shapes out, all twenty-six of them.

3. Cut the cardboard into a wreath shape, making sure to cut out the center.

4. Glue the hand shapes, fingers pointing out, onto the cardboard wreath, one layer at a time.

5. Cut a bow from the red construction paper and glue it to the top or bottom of the wreath.

6. Decorate the "handprint wreath" with green glitter and the bow with red glitter.

7. Allow the wreath to dry, then attach the picture hanger to the back.

What do you remember best about Christmas as a child?

"We didn't see the Christmas tree and presents until the holy evening, December 24. It wasn't Santa Claus who brought the presents— we thought it was Jesus. Rupprecht, Santa's helper, punished the kids when they were not nice.

—Klaus Thiele
San Diego, California

Santa's Questions in a Jar

Supplies

Scissors

Three sheets 8½ x 11-inch white card stock

Santa stamp (no bigger than 1½ x 2½ inches)

Red stamp pad

Green pen

Small clear plastic canister with lid

Christmas fabric

Glue gun

Christmas ribbon

Variation: Computer

Directions

1. Cut thirty strips from the card stock, 1½ x 5 inches each.

2. Fold the strips in half widthwise, to make cards.

3. Stamp the Santa design on the front of each folded card.

4. Use the green pen to write the questions below on the inside of the cards, one question per card.

5. Drop the finished cards into the canister.

6. Lay the fabric on top of the canister lid and cut a square about 2 inches wider than the lid.

7. Center and glue the fabric to the lid.

8. Glue the ribbon around the edge of the lid on top of the fabric. Excess fabric will hang out.

9. Have a child choose a question and talk about it.

Note: This canister is packed with thirty questions kids have always wanted to ask Santa. You may choose to add some of your own or eliminate some.

Variation: Type the questions on the computer and make a game label for the outside of the canister.

Questions to ask Santa

1. What are you going to bring me this year?

2. Do you ever trim your beard or shave?

3. How old are you?

4. How much do you weigh?

5. Do you wear other clothes besides your red Santa suit? What are they?

6. Do you have any of your own kids?

7. What's your favorite football team?

8. What was your favorite subject in school?

9. What kind of grades did you get in school?

10. Do you play any musical instruments? What are they?

11. Do you ski?

12. What do you watch on TV?

13. Does it get cold up in the sleigh while you're flying?

14. Do you get full from drinking and eating all the milk and cookies?

15. How many elves do you have?

16. Do you have any female elves? They always seem to be male in the books.

17. Who's your favorite elf? Why?

18. Who's your favorite reindeer? Why?

19. What's your favorite food? Why?

20. What food do you hate the most?

21. What's your favorite Christmas song?

22. Do you ever get tired of Christmas?

23. How come I see so many Santas around Christmastime? I thought there was only one of you?

24. Do you really give coal to bad kids?

25. Why do you live up at the North Pole and not in Hawaii where it's warm?

26. How many acres of land do you own?

27. Are you happy with the way you are? If there was one thing you could change, what would it be?

28. How do you fit all the presents into your bag?

29. Do you have a middle name?

30. Who cuts your hair, and who curls your beard?

How does Santa know what to bring to you? "We make a list and send it. He sometimes knows what I want even though I didn't write it down—he knows everything."
—Paige and Katie Stevens, Ages 7 and 3 Walled Lake, Michigan

How does Santa know what to bring you? "We're to old, but when we 'believed,' Mom had connections with Santa."
—Theresa and Sean Ayers, Ages 11 and 13 Toledo, Ohio

How does Santa know what to bring you? "By calling him on the phone."
—Emily Howard, Age 12 Denver, Colorado

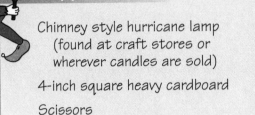

"Santa and Me" Candy Jar

How does Santa know
what to bring you?
"Make a list and
e-mail it."
—Hayley Dell, Age 7½
San Diego, California

Supplies

Chimney style hurricane lamp
(found at craft stores or
wherever candles are sold)

4-inch square heavy cardboard

Scissors

Glue gun

6-inch square white fur

6 x 12-inch white felt

3-inch square black felt

8½ x 12-inch red felt

½-inch pink pom-pom

Needle

Red thread

Red adult sock

Polyester stuffing

1½-inch white pom-pom

Peppermint candy

Directions

1. Trace the bottom of the hurricane lamp onto the cardboard and cut out. Glue the cardboard to the bottom of the lamp.

2. Trace the following pattern pieces onto the white fur and cut out: one beard (pattern piece #1), one right eyebrow (pattern piece #2), one left eyebrow (pattern piece #3), and one mustache (pattern piece #4). Set aside.

3. Trace the following pattern pieces onto the white and black felt and cut out: two white eyes (pattern piece #5) and two black eyes (pattern piece #6). Set aside.

4. Cut out and glue a strip of red felt that fits around the bottom neck of the hurricane lamp.

5. Glue the beard onto the hurricane lamp at the widest point.

6. Cut and glue a thin strip of red felt for a mouth above the beard.

7. Glue the mustache just above the beard showing a small portion of the mouth.

8. Glue the pink pom-pom for a nose just above the mustache.

9. Position and glue the white eyes above the mustache. Then glue the black pupils onto the eyes.

10. Sew a running stitch about 3 inches above the toe area of the sock. Pull the thread to make a loose gather. Then knot and trim any excess thread.

11. Stretch the sock (Santa's hat) around your fingers, and cut and glue a wide strip of white felt around the rim of the sock. It's important to glue the strip while the sock is stretched out, or it will not slide over the lamp.

12. Fill the sock loosely with stuffing.

13. Glue the white pom-pom to the toe of the sock.

14. Fill the hurricane lamp (candy jar) with the peppermint candy.

15. Put Santa's hat on the candy jar. Remove his hat each time to get candy.

#1

#5   #6

#2   #3

#4

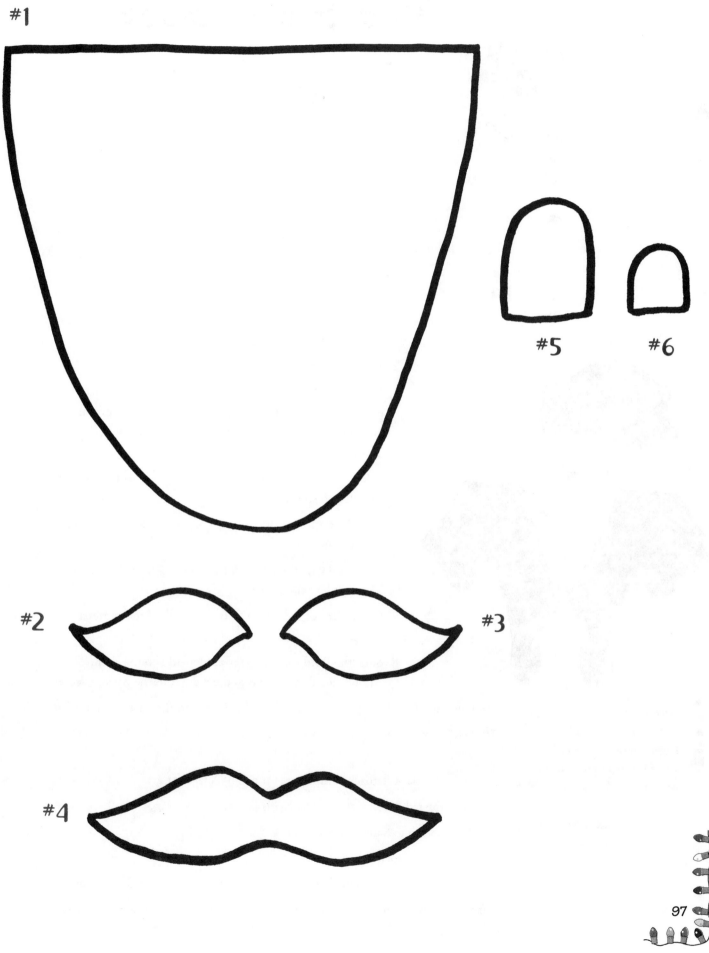

Red Santa Sock

Supplies

Needle

Red thread

Three red baby socks

Scissors

Five ½-inch buttons (any color)

Glue gun

Thin beige fabric

1¾ x 4-inch heavy cardboard

Red felt

White felt

1-inch white pom-pom

White thread

Two black flatback rhinestones

One red flatback rhinestone

Powdered blush

Polyester stuffing

Variation: Larger items, picture hanger (self-adhesive), or wire

Directions

1. With the red thread, sew a running stitch, approximately 1 inch above the toe of one sock, then gather it. Repeat this on a second sock.

2. Sew one button on top of the gathers on each sock.

3. Lay the two socks flat on the table, toes down and heels touching. Glue them together at the heels, then sew on one button to secure. The button does not show in the illustration, as it's under the beard.

4. Fold the top of the socks backward to form Santa's shoulders and glue to secure.

5. Sew one button at the top edge of each sock. You have used the five buttons.

6. Wrap and glue the beige fabric smoothly over the cardboard. This will be Santa's face.

7. Cut a piece of red felt to fit on the back of the cardboard and glue.

8. Slide the third sock over the cardboard about 1 inch. This sock will be Santa's hat. Glue to the red felt in the back to secure.

9. Cut out a ½-inch strip of white felt and glue it around the base of Santa's hat.

10. Sew the white pom-pom to the toe area of the third sock (hat) using the white thread.

11. Glue the black flatback rhinestones onto Santa's face for eyes.

12. Glue the red flatback rhinestone to his face for a nose.

13. Apply blush to Santa's cheeks.

14. Bend his hat forward.

15. Glue stuffing onto Santa's face for a beard and set him on a ledge, sitting.

Tip: There are a variety of fun buttons you can find at sewing and craft stores, even Christmas ones.

Variation: Use adult red socks, but be sure to use larger buttons, cardboard, white felt, pom-poms, and rhinestones. You can also put a picture hanger on the back of the sock so Santa can hang on the wall, or make a wire hanger so Santa can hang on a doorknob.

Elves' Little Hideout

Supplies

Pinking shears

#10 envelope
(any color)

Pencil

Plain white paper

Glue stick

Crayons or markers

Glue gun

1-inch Velcro®

Keebler® E. L. Fudge®
Sandwich Cookies

Directions

1. Lick the envelope closed then cut it in half widthwise. Discard one half or save it to make a second "elves' hideout." The cut edge is the top of the hideout.

2. Fold ½ inch of the left side of the envelope toward the front and then to the back, making a good firm crease line. Do the same on the right side.

3. Fold the bottom of the envelope just like the sides.

4. Trace the elf (pattern piece #1) onto the plain white paper and cut out.

5. With the glue stick, glue the elf to the front center of the envelope just above the bottom crease line.

6. Color the elf.

7. Open the envelope by putting your hand inside it.

8. Flatten the bottom so the envelope stands up like a paper grocery bag. Fold the bottom side flaps under and secure with the glue gun.

9. Fill the bag with elf cookies.

10. Put the Velcro® on the inside of the bag's top, one piece on each side. Close the bag using the Velcro®.

#1

A Gift from Santa

Small rectangular box with gift inside
Red wrapping paper
Scissors
Tape
Yellow construction paper
Wide black ribbon
Black permanent marker

Elf Handprints

Pencil
Twenty-six sheets green construction paper
Scissors
Cardboard
Tacky glue
Red construction paper
Green and red glitter
Picture hanger (self-adhesive)

Don't forget the camera and film

Santa's Questions in a Jar

Scissors
Three sheets 8½ x 11-inch white card stock
Santa stamp (no bigger than 1½ x 2½ inches)
Red stamp pad
Green pen
Small clear plastic canister with lid
Christmas fabric
Glue gun
Christmas ribbon
Variation: Computer

"Santa and Me" Candy Jar

Chimney style hurricane lamp (found at craft stores or wherever candles are sold)
4-inch square heavy cardboard
Scissors
Glue gun
6-inch square white fur
6 x 12-inch white felt

(continued)

Supplies for Santa and His Elves

3-inch square black felt
8½ x 12-inch red felt
½-inch pink pom-pom
Needle
Red thread
Red adult sock
Polyester stuffing
1½-inch white pom-pom
Peppermint candy

Red Santa Sock

Needle
Red thread
Three red baby socks
Scissors
Five ½-inch buttons (any color)
Glue gun
Thin beige fabric
1¾ x 4-inch heavy cardboard
Red felt
White felt
1-inch white pom-pom
White thread

(continued)

Two black flatback rhinestones
One red flatback rhinestone
Powdered blush
Polyester stuffing
Variation: Larger items, picture hanger (self-adhesive), or wire

Elves' Little Hideout

Pinking shears
#10 envelope (any color)
Pencil
Plain white paper
Glue stick
Crayons or markers
Glue gun
1-inch Velcro®
Keebler® E. L. Fudge® Sandwich Cookies

Reindeer Sucker

Supplies

Scissors

12-inch brown pipe cleaner

Glue gun

Green plastic spoon

Two 7mm moving eyes

½-inch red pom-pom

8 inches ¼" red ribbon

Wrapped round sucker

Directions

1. Cut the pipe cleaner into two 3-inch pieces and one 6-inch piece.

2. Slightly bend the 6-inch piece of pipe cleaner and glue the center to the inside of the spoon bowl to form part of the antler.

3. Twist and attach each 3-inch piece of pipe cleaner, one to each side of the 6-inch piece, to form the rest of the antler.

4. Glue the moving eyes to the outside of the spoon bowl.

5. Glue the red pom-pom (reindeer nose) just below the eyes.

6. Tie the red ribbon into a bow around the spoon handle just under the bowl.

7. Glue the wrapped sucker to the "inside" of the spoon.

Variation: Use different colored spoons, pipe cleaners, pom-poms, and/or ribbons for a variety of looks.

Craft Stick Reindeer

Supplies

Glue gun

Three craft sticks

½-inch red pom-pom

Two 12mm moving eyes

6 inches ¼" red ribbon

7 inches ⅛" red ribbon

Directions

1. Glue two craft sticks together to form the letter "V."

2. Glue the red pom-pom onto the craft sticks at the bottom of the "V."

3. Glue one moving eye to the center of each craft stick.

4. Glue the third craft stick across the "V" about an inch above the eyes.

5. Tie the ¼" red ribbon into a bow and glue it to the center of the horizontal stick.

6. Loop and glue the ⅛" red ribbon to the backside of the reindeer to form a handle.

Rudolph and His Reindeer

Candy Cane Reindeer

Supplies

Supplies for Version 1:

Scissors

12-inch green or brown pipe cleaner

Ruler

Candy cane (unwrapped)

Glue gun

Two 6mm moving eyes

¼-inch red pom-pom

Supplies for Version 2:

Glue gun

Two multicolored candy canes (unwrapped)

Brown yarn

Scissors

Two 8mm moving eyes

½-inch red pom-pom

8 inches ⅛" red ribbon

Directions for Version 1

1. Cut the pipe cleaner into two 3-inch pieces and one 6-inch piece.

2. Twist and bend the 6-inch piece around the curved part of the candy cane to form part of the antlers.

3. Twist one 3-inch piece to each end of the 6-inch piece to finish the antlers.

4. Glue both moving eyes and the red pom-pom (nose) to the curved part of the candy cane for the reindeer face.

Directions for Version 2

1. Glue the candy canes together so the "hooks" are pointed out.

2. Glue the beginning of the yarn at the bottom of the canes and wind it around the canes, covering the canes, to the base of the hooks. Cut and glue the end of the yarn to the backside of the canes.

3. Glue the moving eyes onto the yarn on the front at the base of the hooks.

4. Glue the pom-pom (nose) under the eyes for the reindeer nose.

5. Tie the ribbon into a bow and glue it to the front bottom of the reindeer.

Rudolph the Reindeer Pencil

Supplies

Brown wood stain

Oval wooden "cowee" bead with 10mm hole

Pencil

Glue gun

Two 7mm moving eyes

¼-inch red pom-pom

Scissors

6-inch brown pipe cleaner

Small plastic sprig of holly and berries

Paper

Directions

1. Stain the bead brown and let it dry.

2. Push the bead (reindeer head) over the pencil's eraser.

3. Glue the moving eyes to the head on the front, then the red pom-pom (reindeer nose) under the eyes.

4. Cut the pipe cleaner into two 3-inch pieces for antlers. Twist one end of each to form antler "hooks."

5. Glue the other ends into the top of the bead. Bend the antlers out.

6. Glue a sprig of holly and berries into the bead between the antlers.

7. Now write to Santa with the pencil. See sample letters at the beginning of the book.

Reindeer Pin

Supplies

12-inch 15mm brown pipe cleaner

Glue gun

½-inch red pom-pom

Two 7mm moving eyes

6 inches ¼" Christmas ribbon

1-inch pin back

Directions

1. Bend one-third of the pipe cleaner to form a loop and twist to secure.

2. Bend the second third into another loop, and twist to secure at the same place you've secured the first loop.

3. Bend the last third into a loop, twisting to secure in the middle of what is now a clover-shape. (A three-leaf, not the lucky four-leaf!)

4. Shape the "clover" to look like the illustration, one "leaf" into a reindeer face and the other two into ears.

5. Glue the red pom-pom (reindeer nose) and the moving eyes to the face as shown in the illustration.

6. Tie the ribbon into a bow and glue above the eyes where all three loops meet.

7. Glue the pin to the back of the reindeer.

Reindeer Footprint

Supplies

Wax paper

Tan acrylic paint

8½ x 11-inch white card stock

Plastic tub of warm water, soap, and towel

Red acrylic paint

Paint brush

Brown acrylic paint

Directions

1. Place a 12-inch square of wax paper on the floor, then pour tan acrylic paint in the center, enough to cover the bottom of your child's foot.

2. Place the card stock on the floor near the paint.

3. Remove the child's sock and shoe from his right foot and have him, with your help, place his foot firmly into the paint, then onto the middle of the card stock. This will be the reindeer's head. Immediately wash and dry the foot and let the child put his sock and shoe back on. Discard the wax paper.

4. Squirt some more paint onto another square of wax paper and have the child place his right hand in the paint, then have him put it on the card stock to the right side of the toes for reindeer antlers. Squirt some more paint onto the wax paper and repeat with his left handprint to the left of the toes. Immediately wash and dry his hands. Discard the wax paper.

5. Use a smaller piece of wax paper and squirt a little dab of red paint on it.

6. Have the child place the tip of his thumb in the red paint, then on the "heel" of the reindeer's face for a nose. Wash off the thumb.

7. Paint two eyes on the reindeer's face with the brown paint.

Note: You can always do this right by a bathtub so it's easier to wash as you go.

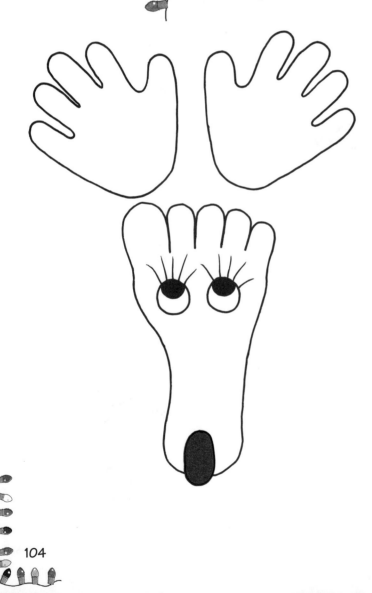

Supplies for Rudolph and His Reindeer

Reindeer Sucker

Scissors
12-inch brown pipe
    cleaner
Glue gun
Green plastic spoon
Two 7mm moving eyes
½-inch red pom-pom
8 inches ¼" red ribbon
Wrapped round
    sucker

Craft Stick Reindeer

Glue gun
Three craft sticks
½-inch red pom-pom
Two 12mm moving eyes
6 inches ¼" red ribbon
7 inches ⅛" red ribbon

Candy Cane Reindeer

Supplies for Version 1:
Scissors
12-inch green or
    brown pipe cleaner
Ruler
Candy cane (unwrapped)
Glue gun
Two 6mm moving eyes
¼-inch red pom-pom

Supplies for Version 2:
Glue gun
Two multicolored candy
    canes (unwrapped)
Brown yarn
Scissors
Two 8mm moving eyes
½-inch red pom-pom
8 inches ⅛" red ribbon

Don't forget the
camera and film

Rudolph the Reindeer Pencil

Brown wood stain
Oval wooden "cowee"
    bead with 10mm hole
Pencil
Glue gun
Two 7mm moving eyes
¼-inch red pom-pom
Scissors
6-inch brown pipe
    cleaner
Small plastic sprig
    of holly and berries
Paper

Reindeer Pin

12-inch 15mm brown
    pipe cleaner
Glue gun
½-inch red pom-pom
Two 7mm moving eyes
6 inches ¼" Christmas
    ribbon
1-inch pin back

Reindeer Footprint

Wax paper
Tan acrylic paint
8½ x 11-inch white
    card stock
Plastic tub of warm
    water, soap, and
    towel
Red acrylic paint
Paint brush
Brown acrylic paint

Lunchbag Angel

Supplies

White lunchbag

White tissue paper

30 inches opal-colored metallic twisted craft paper

Scissors

Glue gun

3-inch round Styrofoam® ball

Spanish moss

10-inch white doily

Twist tie

Black permanent marker

Directions

1. Stuff the lunchbag with the tissue paper until half full for the angel's body. Make sure the bag's bottom is flat so it can stand up.

2. Unfold the twisted craft paper, then flatten and smooth with your hands. You may use either side, just be consistent.

3. Gather the bag's edges and tie a bow around it with the craft paper for the angel's neck. Trim off any extra paper.

4. Open the bag's top and glue the Styrofoam® ball into the opening for the head.

5. Glue Spanish moss to the top of the ball for hair.

6. Fold the doily accordion-style, then bend the twist tie around its center.

7. Glue the doily to the back of the angel's neck, and fan it out for wings.

8. Using the permanent marker, draw eyes and an oval mouth on the angel to make it sing.

Easy-to-Make Angel

Supplies

Natural, basket-style disposable coffee filter, 8 to 12 cup size

Glue gun

White, basket-style disposable coffee filter, 1 to 4 cup size

1 x ⅛-inch wooden circle

Black permanent marker

Powdered blush (red)

Tacky glue

Gold glitter

Mini-spring clothespin (found at craft stores)

Directions

1. Fold the natural coffee filter in half. With the fold side up, slide the top layer up a little. Gather in the center and glue.

2. Gather the white filter in the center and glue it to the center of the folded edge of the natural filter

3. Glue the wooden circle on the top center of the white filter for the angel's face.

4. Dot two eyes on the face with the black permanent marker.

5. Rub the tip of your finger onto the blush then onto the face for cheeks.

6. Make a halo by squeezing out a small curve of glue above the angel's eyes and sprinkling it with glitter. Let dry.

7. Glue the clothespin onto the back of the angel so you can hang it anywhere.

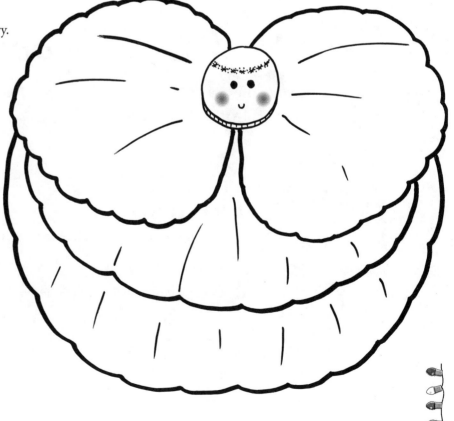

Your Angel's Handprint

Supplies

Iron

7-inch square muslin fabric

Red acrylic paint

Paper plate

Green permanent marker

6-inch wooden embroidery hoop

9 inches ⅛" green ribbon

Directions

1. Iron the fabric flat.

2. Pour the red paint onto the paper plate.

3. Help the child place his hand into the paint then onto the center of the fabric. He should wash his hand immediately. Let the fabric dry overnight.

4. Using the permanent marker, write "My Angel (the child's name)" below the handprint. Below, write "Christmas (the current year)."

5. Stretch and insert the fabric into the embroidery hoop. Trim any excess fabric, such as the corners.

6. Loop and tie the ribbon to the screw on the embroidery hoop for a hook.

My Angel Michelle
Christmas 2000

Angel Spoon Ornament

Supplies

Red permanent marker

White plastic spoon

Glue gun

Yellow shredded paper

8 inches 3" gold metallic ribbon

4 inches fishing line

Directions

1. Draw a face on the "inside" bowl of the spoon.

2. Glue shredded paper to the top of the spoon for hair.

3. Tie a bow around the neck of the spoon with the gold metallic ribbon.

4. Loop and glue the fishing line to the back neck of the spoon to hang it.

Singing Angel

Supplies

- 2-inch terra cotta clay pot
- Paintbrush
- Silver acrylic paint
- 1¼-inch wooden "head" bead
- Flesh-tone acrylic paint
- Glue gun
- Spanish moss
- Black permanent marker
- Powdered blush (red)
- 3 inches thin silver garland

Directions

1. Paint the outside and bottom of the clay pot silver and let dry.

2. Paint the wooden bead (head) flesh-tone and let it dry.

3. Glue the head to the bottom of the clay pot.

4. Glue Spanish moss on the head for hair.

5. Use the black permanent marker to draw the angel's eyes and an oval "singing mouth."

6. Rub the tip of your finger onto the blush then onto the face for cheeks.

7. Form a halo with the silver garland, and glue it to the angel's head.

What is a good gift? What was the best gift you ever gave?
"Something that will make your best friend cry. I gave my friend Sandy an angel fountain, because it was her first Christmas without her two-year-old daughter, Mallory, who had passed away. My friend thinks of her daughter as an angel so collects them. Giving her this gift meant so much to me because I knew in my heart what it meant to her. It made my Christmas holiday special."

—MaryAnn Stevens
Walled Lake, Michigan

Stand-up Angel

Supplies

24 inches gray twisted craft paper

Paper cone cup (used with
   water cooler)

Scissors

Glue gun

15 inches ½" white lace

1½-inch wooden bead

Spanish moss

Small flower appliqué

Directions

1. Unfold the twisted craft paper, then flatten and smooth with your hands. You may use either side, just be consistent.

2. Stand the paper cone cup on a table or countertop. Wrap, cut, and glue the craft paper around the cup starting at the tip and going down to the widest part, for the angel's dress.

3. Glue about 10 inches of lace around the bottom of the dress.

4. Place the wooden bead (head) over the tip of the cup.

5. Cut one thin strip from the craft paper, about 6 inches long. Glue the center just under the bead in the back and wrap the sides to the front for arms. Glue the angel's hands together.

6. Make a bow from the craft paper, scrunch it slightly in the center and secure with a thin piece of craft paper. Glue the bow to the back of the angel's dress for wings.

7. Glue Spanish moss on the top of the bead (head) for hair.

8. Wrap and glue the remaining lace around the angel's neck to form a collar.

9. Glue the small flower appliqué onto the front of the collar.

Lunchbag Angel

White lunchbag
White tissue paper
30 inches opal-
  colored metallic
  twisted craft paper
Scissors
Glue gun
3-inch round
  Styrofoam® ball
Spanish moss
10-inch white doily
Twist tie
Black permanent
  marker

Don't forget the
camera and film

Easy-to-
Make Angel

Natural, basket-style
  disposable coffee
  filter, 8 to 12 cup size
Glue gun
White, basket-style
  disposable coffee
  filter, 1 to 4 cup size
1 x ⅛-inch wooden circle
Black permanent marker
Powdered blush (red)
Tacky glue
Gold glitter
Mini-spring clothespin
  (found at craft
  stores)

Your Angel's
Handprint

Iron
7-inch square muslin
  fabric
Red acrylic paint
Paper plate
Green permanent
  marker
6-inch wooden
  embroidery hoop
9 inches ⅛" green
  ribbon

Supplies for
I Believe in Angels

Angel Spoon
Ornament

Red permanent marker
White plastic spoon
Glue gun
Yellow shredded paper
8 inches 3" gold
  metallic ribbon
4 inches fishing line

Singing
Angel

2-inch terra cotta
  clay pot
Paintbrush
Silver acrylic paint
1¼-inch wooden "head"
  bead
Flesh-tone acrylic paint
Glue gun
Spanish moss
Black permanent marker
Powdered blush (red)
3 inches thin silver
  garland

Stand-up
Angel

24 inches gray twisted
  craft paper
Paper cone cup
  (used with water
  cooler)
Scissors
Glue gun
15 inches ½" white lace
1½-inch wooden bead
Spanish moss
Small flower appliqué

Christmas Here, There, and Everywhere — Global Celebrations

Thomas Smith, a candy maker, started making crackers (fireworks that POP! when you pull both ends) in 1844 after a visit to Paris where he learned how the French wrapped sugarcoated almonds in colored paper. He invented a friction cap strip on the cracker, which makes a popping sound when the ends are pulled open.

Christmas Cracker
Great Britain

Supplies

Scissors
Paper
Pen

Candy
Coins
Christmas trinkets
Toilet paper tube

Christmas wrapping paper
Tape
Curling ribbon

Directions

1. Cut strips of paper, then write Christmas wishes on each.

2. Insert the paper wishes, candy, coins, and Christmas trinkets into the toilet paper tube.

3. Wrap the toilet paper tube with the Christmas paper, leaving excess paper on both ends, and tape to secure.

4. Twist the paper at the ends and secure with curling ribbon. Curl the ribbon with scissors.

5. Put one cracker by each dinner plate on Christmas Eve or Day. Open before eating.

Design a Christmas Seal
Denmark

Supplies

Sticker paper (found at craft stores)
Crayons or markers

In 1904, the first Christmas seals, decorative stamps for letters and packages, were designed and sold in Denmark. The proceeds went to fight tuberculosis.

Directions

1. Draw and color an original Christmas design that you think would look good on a letter or package at Christmastime.

2. Cut out and stick on a letter or package.

Rutabaga Candle
Ireland

Supplies

Knife

Rutabaga
(Swedish turnip)

Emergency candle
(5-inch, found at
grocery stores)

Scissors

Colored paper
(any color)

Glue

Large plastic sprigs
of holly and berries

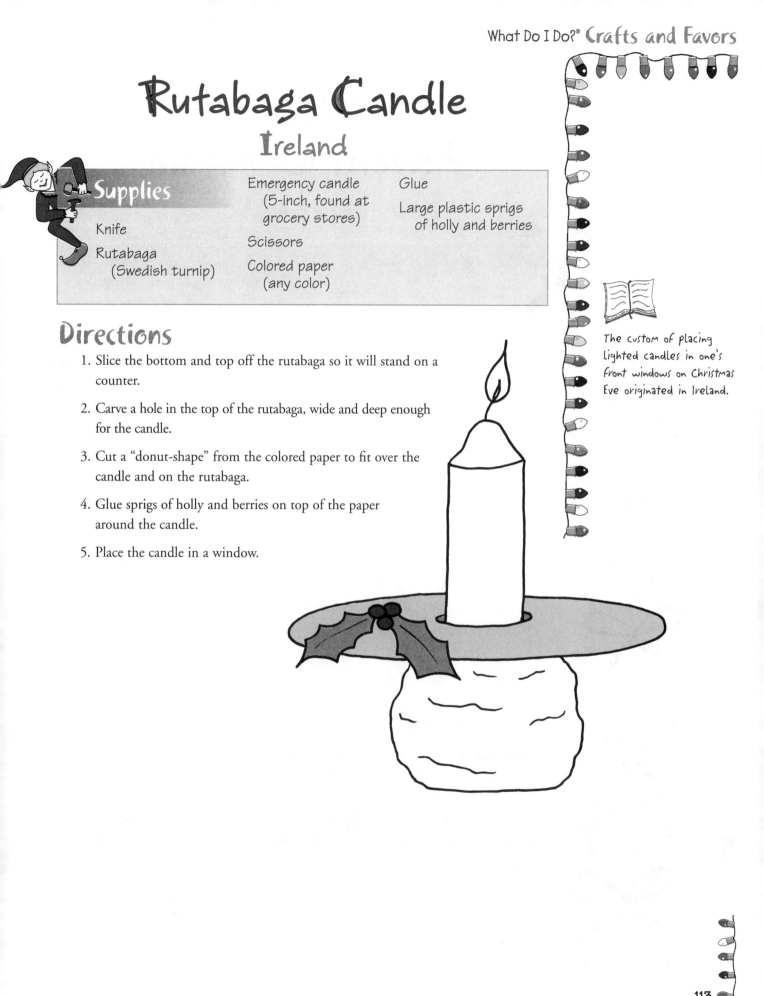

Directions

1. Slice the bottom and top off the rutabaga so it will stand on a counter.

2. Carve a hole in the top of the rutabaga, wide and deep enough for the candle.

3. Cut a "donut-shape" from the colored paper to fit over the candle and on the rutabaga.

4. Glue sprigs of holly and berries on top of the paper around the candle.

5. Place the candle in a window.

The custom of placing lighted candles in one's front windows on Christmas Eve originated in Ireland.

Hanging Candy Advent Calendar

In Anticipation of Christmas

Supplies

Twenty-five Christmas candies (individually wrapped)

Clear plastic wrap

Scissors

Red yarn

Green yarn

Variation 1: Poster board, crayons or markers, stapler or tape, and picture hanger (self-adhesive)

Variation 2: Wooden Christmas cut-out (found at craft stores), stain or paint, paintbrush, picture hanger (self-adhesive), and stapler

Directions

1. Roll out the plastic wrap on a long table.

2. Lay the candies down the center of the wrap, leaving a 2-inch space between the pieces and a 3-inch space at the top and bottom of the plastic wrap.

3. Roll the long sides of the plastic wrap around the candy, careful not to let the candy shift.

4. Cut twenty-six pieces of yarn each into 8-inch pieces, thirteen red and thirteen green.

5. Tie a piece of yarn between the pieces of candy and at each end, then tie into bows.

6. Loop and tie an additional piece of yarn to one end for the top of the calendar. Use this to hang the calendar on the wall or door.

Variation 1: Draw a Christmas design on the poster board. Color it, cut it out, and staple or tape the top of the candy to the bottom of the poster board. Then attach the picture hanger to the back.

Variation 2: Choose a wooden Christmas cut-out from the craft store, then stain or paint it. Attach the picture hanger to the back. Staple or tape the top of the candy to the back of the wood.

Star of David
To Celebrate Hanukkah

Supplies

White poster board
11 feet cording (any color)

Scissors
Tacky glue
Cellophane wrap
(assorted colors)

Directions

1. Form a six-star pattern on the poster board with the cording: two equilateral 10-inch triangles, one on top of the other, only upside down. When you are happy with your Star of David, glue it to the poster board.

2. Cut pieces of cellophane, assorted sizes, and randomly glue them inside the star, careful not to cover the cording.

3. Cut out the star.

4. Repeat steps #1 and #2 on the backside of the poster board.

5. Cut an 8-inch piece of cording, make a loop, and glue it to any point of the star for a hanger.

6. Hang your Star of David near a window for a stained glass effect.

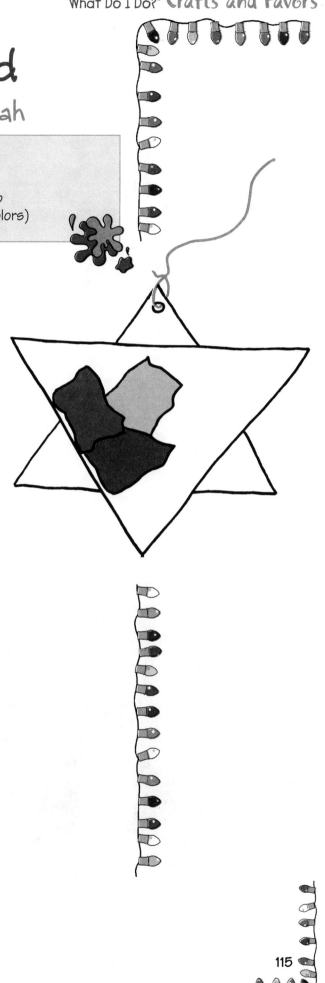

Nativity Scene
Italy

Supplies

Craft sticks

Tacky glue
Crayons or markers
White paper

Scissors
Styrofoam®
Spanish moss

Directions

1. With craft sticks, build and glue a stable, with three sides and a roof, at least 6 inches tall, 6 inches wide, and 6 inches deep. Leave some craft sticks for the nativity characters.

2. Draw the following people on the white paper, no taller than 3 inches or wider than 2 inches: Baby Jesus, Mary, and Joseph in a manger. Also, add a few other characters and animals of your choice. Color them, then cut them out.

3. Glue the figures to craft sticks and let dry.

4. Stick the figures into small pieces of Styrofoam® and arrange them in the stable.

5. Spread Spanish moss around the bottom of the stick figures, covering the Styrofoam®.

Christmas Cracker
Great Britain

Scissors
Paper
Pen
Candy
Coins
Christmas trinkets
Toilet paper tube
Christmas wrapping
  paper
Tape
Curling ribbon

Design a Christmas Seal
Denmark

Sticker paper
  (found at craft
  stores)
Crayons or markers

Rutabaga Candle
Ireland

Knife
Rutabaga
  (Swedish turnip)
Emergency candle
  (5-inch, found at
  grocery stores)
Scissors
Colored paper
  (any color)
Glue
Large plastic sprigs
  of holly and berries

Don't forget the
camera and film

Hanging Candy Advent Calendar
In Anticipation of Christmas

Twenty-five Christmas
  candies (individually
  wrapped)
Clear plastic wrap
Scissors
Red yarn
Green yarn
Variation 1: Poster
  board, crayons or
  markers, stapler or
  tape, and picture
  hanger (self-adhesive)
Variation 2: Wooden
  Christmas cut-out
  (found at craft
  stores), stain or
  paint, paintbrush,
  picture hanger
  (self- adhesive),
  and stapler

Supplies for Christmas Here, There, and Everywhere — Global Celebrations

Star of David
To Celebrate Hanukkah

White poster board
11 feet cording
  (any color)
Scissors
Tacky glue
Cellophane wrap
  (assorted colors)

Nativity Scene
Italy

Craft sticks
Tacky glue
Crayons or markers
White paper
Scissors
Styrofoam®
Spanish moss

CHAPTER 4
Holiday Goodies

Helpful Hints for Holiday Goodies

1. Some of the goodies require preparation before a party, so read the directions well in advance.

2. To help eliminate Christmas stress, prepare as much of the recipe as possible days or weeks before the party. Most Christmas cookies can be baked and frozen months ahead.

3. Any goody requiring whipped cream is best made immediately before serving to avoid flops.

4. Stores in your area may not carry needed supplies or ingredients, or you may just have trouble finding them. Don't fret, use the Internet! Or substitute an equal or better choice.

5. A gumdrop is also called a spice drop.

6. Most of the recipes in this chapter are for children and adults to make together, unless you're trying to keep the goody a surprise.

7. Some recipes, such as Santa's Candy Sleigh, found on page 136, or Santa's Chimneys, found on page 140, may look difficult to make but are very easy. Give them a try!

8. When giving a party for lots of guests, buffet lines work well for adults and children at least eight years old.

9. Serve at least two different Holiday Goodies, so you're sure to please everyone.

10. When planning for school parties, check with the teacher concerning any food allergies the students may have. Some children are allergic to peanut butter, so don't serve Santa's Chocolate Sleigh Bell Cookies, found on page 137. Even the smell may affect some kids.

11. When adding peanut butter or shortening to measuring cups, first rinse the cups with water. The moisture helps the sticky mixture slide out easier.

12. Always, always have extra goodies (for school parties) for the teacher, parent helpers, and siblings. Give janitors any leftovers. They really appreciate it.

13. Wash your hands before making any goodies. December *is* during the flu and cold season.

14. Cookie decorating parties are always fun for adults, children, and groups such as Girl Scout troops.

15. A roll of cookie dough (found at grocery stores) works great for cut-out cookies.

16. Instead of using canned frosting, use a favorite recipe and tint the frosting with Wilton® icing colors.

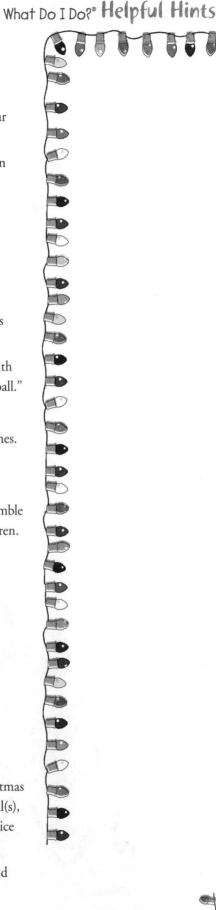

17. When using Royal Icing, found on pages 136 and 148, be sure to cover your bowl with a damp towel when not "frosting."

18. Don't forget frosting in a tube when you want to decorate but are limited on time and equipment.

19. If you're short on time and need an easy, cute dessert idea, buy store-made frosted cupcakes and add a few touches of your own to decorate them. See Singing Angel Cupcake, found on page 149.

20. Just got an invitation to a party? Want to bring something? Cut cheese into squares and insert a Christmas toothpick.

21. A combination of green olives and cherry tomatoes on a small skewer makes for a nice Christmas appetizer.

22. For an easy Christmas goody, wrap a popcorn ball in plastic wrap, secure with red and green curling ribbon, and attach a note card saying, "Crunchy Snowball."

23. Let those little elves (your children) help in the kitchen.

24. Use Christmas cookie cutters to cut out waffles, toast, or bread for sandwiches.

25. Turn off the TV and listen to Christmas music while making goodies, even sing along.

26. While cookies are baking, make a craft or play a game from this book. Unscramble Eskimo Christmas Food, found on page 68 is fun for both adults and children.

27. Most of the items in this chapter can be given as gifts. Teachers especially appreciate home-baked goodies because they don't have time to bake for themselves. Here are some ways you could package your goodies, but read the directions to see if they need time to cool or harden first:

    • Wrap with red cellophane
    • Display on a Christmas plate
    • Set in a basket lined with a Christmas towel
    • Store in Christmas tins
    • Place on a new cookie sheet
    • Put in Christmas fabric sacks

    Tie your packages with ribbons, raffia (found at craft stores), strips of Christmas fabric, or pieces of rope. Also add any of the following: cookie cutter, jingle bell(s), small bag of candy, recipe, ornament, Christmas pencil, or note card with nice thoughts or memories about the recipient.

28. One of Santa's favorite snacks is Santa's Chocolate Sleigh Bell Cookies, found on page 137. Leave him a full plate.

29. Santa's reindeer also want goodies. Throw mini carrots in your yard just before going to bed on Christmas Eve.

30. Traditions are fun, so pick a holiday goody to make each year. Mine, if you couldn't tell by now, is Santa's Chocolate Sleigh Bell Cookies.

The Yummiest Candy Christmas Tree Ever

Ingredients and Supplies

Makes enough for a party

Toothpicks
(one per two gumdrops)

Approximately 185 gumdrops
(assorted colors)

3 x 6-inch Styrofoam® cone

Variation 1: All green gumdrops

Variation 2: Red, green, and assorted-colored gumdrops

Variation 3: Lettuce, baby sweet pickles, green and/or black olives, and radishes

Variation 4: Wrapped peppermint candies

Optional: Star eraser

Directions

1. Break the toothpicks in half.

2. Stick one gumdrop onto the *pointed end* of each toothpick half.
   Caution: Do not stick the broken ends of the toothpicks into the candy!

3. Stick the broken ends of the toothpicks into the Styrofoam® cone, starting at the bottom and working your way to the top until the entire cone is covered.

Variation 1: Make the whole tree green. You can buy all green gumdrops at Christmastime, usually in the bulk section of the grocery store.

Variation 2: Using red gumdrops, design a red ribbon swirling down and around the Christmas tree. Fill in with green gumdrops, randomly adding assorted-colored gumdrops throughout the tree for lights and ornaments.

Variation 3: Using toothpicks, cover the tree first with lettuce, then baby sweet pickles, green and/or black olives, and radishes.

Variation 4: Cover the tree with wrapped peppermint candies, sticking the toothpicks through the edge of the wrappers.

Optional: A star eraser would make a good tree topper; just don't let anyone eat it.

Individual Candy Cane Cakes

Ingredients and Supplies

Makes 4 cakes

Cake mix (any flavor)

9 x 13-inch pan

Cake rack

Knife

16-ounce can white frosting

Scissors

Red shoestring licorice (soft)

Optional: Cutting board (big enough for cake)

Directions

1. Using the directions on the box, bake the cake in the 9 x 13-inch pan. Let cool on the cake rack.

2. Loosen the sides of the cake with the knife and flip it onto the rack or a cutting board. Cut the cake into four sections.

3. Cut a candy cane shape from each of the four sections.

4. Frost each candy cane cake.

5. Cut the red shoestring licorice to make candy cane stripes, then decorate the top and sides of each cake.

Tip: Freeze the cake before frosting. You won't get as many crumbs.

What family traditions do you have for the holidays?

"The children and I make a gingerbread house each year. I make all the pieces, and the kids are in charge of helping put it together. (My daughter Sarah got this bright idea a couple of years ago that a blow dryer would help the icing cement faster, and it does!) Then the kids decorate the house with an assortment of candies. We add small trees from a cake decorations store, and cars, buried in the snow, plus extras such as a garage."
—Barb Scott
Bucyrus, Ohio

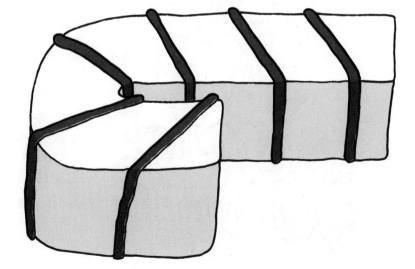

Creamy Deviled Egg Christmas Tree

Ingredients and Supplies

Makes 17 deviled eggs

Nine hard-boiled eggs

Knife

Small spoon

Mixer and bowl

5 heaping tablespoons mayonnaise

½ teaspoon salt

¼ teaspoon pepper

¾ teaspoon prepared mustard

Green food coloring

Decorating bag

Coupler

Decorating tip #22

Lettuce

Cookie sheet

Bacon bits or crushed chestnuts

Optional: Paprika, pimento, or green onions

Directions

1. Peel the eggs, then slice them in half lengthwise.

2. Scoop all the egg yolks into the mixing bowl.

3. Add the mayonnaise, salt, pepper, and prepared mustard to the egg yolks. Mix until very creamy with no lumps.

4. Add a few drops of green food coloring to the egg mixture and beat until well blended. Add food coloring until you get your choice of green.

5. Put the egg mixture into the decorating bag with the coupler and tip #22.

6. Squeeze the green egg mixture into the hollow egg whites.

7. Lay lettuce on the cookie sheet, then arrange the creamy deviled eggs into a tree shape starting with one egg in the first row, then two in the second row, and so on with five eggs in the fifth row. Under the five eggs, add two eggs for the tree trunk. You will have one egg left, so hurry and eat it before anyone sees you!

8. Sprinkle tiny amounts of bacon bits or crushed chestnuts onto the eggs.

Optional: Sprinkle the eggs with paprika, pimento, or green onion slices.

Chewy Christmas Trees

Ingredients and Supplies

Makes 12 trees

Butter or margarine

Cookie sheet

Paper towel

Christmas tree cookie cutter (outline only)

Twelve fruit slice candies

Sharp-tipped knife

Kellogg's™ Rice Krispies® cereal

Measuring cups

Marshmallows

Large saucepan

Spoon or spatula

Green food coloring

Decorating Décors (fruit-flavored)

Directions

1. Butter the cookie sheet and set aside.

2. Lightly butter a clean counter using a paper towel.

3. Butter the cookie cutter.

4. Flatten a fruit slice candy with your fingers, then place it on the buttered counter. Flatten it more with the palm of your hand if needed.

5. Butter the tip of your knife and cut a star from the candy.

6. Repeat steps #4 and #5 eleven more times and set the stars aside. Butter your knife for each slice if the candy tugs.

7. Make a batch of Rice Krispies Treats® using the recipe on the cereal box, except before adding the cereal, put a few drops of green food coloring in the marshmallow mixture and stir well.

8. While warm, press the mixture onto the cookie sheet and cut out twelve tree shapes with the buttered cookie cutter. Work quickly, reshaping the trees and re-buttering the cookie cutter as needed.

9. Place a fruit star on the top of each tree and stick Decorating Décors throughout the tree for lights and ornaments.

Variation: Make tree cone shapes instead of using a cookie cutter and decorate as in step #9.

Tip: It would be helpful to have a second person decorating the trees before they harden.

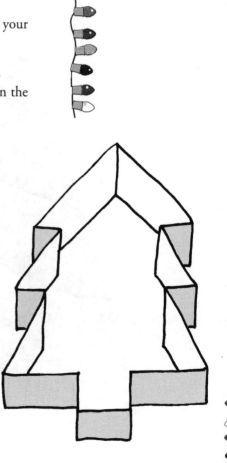

Sugar Cone Christmas Tree

Ingredients and Supplies

Makes 4 trees

Four sugar cones

Four small sturdy red paper plates

16-ounce can green frosting

Three decorating bags

Three decorating couplers

Decorating tips #2, #21, and #32

16-ounce can yellow frosting

16-ounce can red frosting

10-ounces colored nonpareils

Twenty sugar cubes

Directions

1. Turn a sugar cone upside down in the center of a plate.

2. Put the green frosting into a decorating bag with a coupler and tip #21.

3. Squeeze the frosting out of the bag onto the bottom of the cone, pulling toward you and down at the same time to make tree branches.

4. Continue around the bottom then work your way to the top until the whole cone is covered.

5. Put the yellow frosting in a decorating bag with a coupler and tip #32.

6. Squeeze a yellow star on top of the tree.

7. Put red frosting in the third decorating bag with a coupler and tip #2.

8. Apply garland to the tree by making a thin red line diagonally and around the tree, starting at the bottom and working your way to the top.

9. Sprinkle the colored nonpareils all over the tree.

10. Repeat steps #1 to #9 three more times.

11. Use the red frosting to make ribbons and bows on the sugar cubes for presents. Put five under each tree.

Pretzel Trees

Ingredients and Supplies

Makes 3 trees

Three pretzel rods

Knife

2 ounces Wilton®
White Candy Melts™
or white chocolate

Saucepan or shallow
microwavable dish

Spoon or spatula

10 ounces Decorating
Décors green
sugar crystals

Wax paper

Directions

1. Break each pretzel rod into four equal pieces. Set aside three of the end pieces for the tree trunks. Use the knife to carve all the ends of the other nine pieces into "corner angles." (See step #5.)

2. Melt the candy over low heat in the saucepan, stirring constantly, or in a microwave.

3. Empty the green sugar onto wax paper.

4. One at a time, roll three "carved" pretzel pieces in the candy, then immediately in the sugar.

5. Lay the three pieces into a tree shape on another piece of wax paper. Dab more melted candy at each corner to secure pieces.

6. Attach an "uncarved" pretzel piece (trunk) to the bottom of the tree with a dab of candy.

7. Sprinkle green sugar on any areas uncovered.

8. Repeat steps #4 through #7 to make the other two Pretzel Trees.

9. Let the trees harden for about 1 hour before carefully peeling them from the wax paper.

Note: Make lots of these trees—they're delicious.

The Yummiest Candy Christmas Tree Ever

Toothpicks (one per two gumdrops)
Approximately 185 gumdrops (assorted colors)
3 x 6-inch Styrofoam® cone
Variation 1: All green gumdrops
Variation 2: Red, green, and assorted-colored gumdrops
Variation 3: Lettuce, baby sweet pickles, green and/or black olives, and radishes
Variation 4: Wrapped peppermint candies
Optional: Star eraser

Individual Candy Cane Cakes

Cake mix (any flavor)
9 x 13-inch pan
Cake rack
Knife
16-ounce can white frosting

(continued)

Scissors
Red shoestring licorice (soft)
Optional: Cutting board (big enough for cake)

Creamy Deviled Egg Christmas Tree

Nine hard-boiled eggs
Knife
Small spoon
Mixer and bowl
5 heaping tablespoons mayonnaise
½ teaspoon salt
¼ teaspoon pepper
¾ teaspoon prepared mustard
Green food coloring
Decorating bag
Coupler
Decorating tip #22
Lettuce
Cookie sheet
Bacon bits or crushed chestnuts
Optional: Paprika, pimento, or green onions

Chewy Christmas Trees

Butter or margarine
Cookie sheet
Paper towel
Christmas tree cookie cutter (outline only)
Twelve fruit slice candies
Sharp-tipped knife
Kellogg's™ Rice Krispies® cereal
Measuring cups
Marshmallows
Large saucepan
Spoon or spatula
Green food coloring
Decorating Décors (fruit-flavored)

Sugar Cone Christmas Tree

Four sugar cones
Four small sturdy red paper plates
16-ounce can green frosting
Three decorating bags

(continued)

Ingredients and Supplies for Christmas Trees, Stockings, and Candy Canes

Three decorating couplers
Decorating tips #2, #21, and #32
16-ounce can yellow frosting
16-ounce can red frosting
10-ounces colored nonpareils
Twenty sugar cubes

Pretzel Trees

Three pretzel rods
Knife
2 ounces Wilton® White Candy Melts™ or white chocolate
Saucepan or shallow microwavable dish
Spoon or spatula
10 ounces Decorating Décors green sugar crystals
Wax paper

Snowman Donut

Ingredients and Supplies

Makes one snowman

Powdered donut hole

Powdered bite-size donut

Powdered large donut

Knife

Two large black gumdrops

Black decorating gel

Two pretzel sticks

Candy corn

Directions

1. Stack the donuts and donut hole, largest to smallest, to make the snowman.

2. Slice ¼ inch off the bottom of one black gumdrop. Flatten the ¼-inch piece of gumdrop with your hand and stick it on the donut hole (head) with decorating gel.

3. Center the second gumdrop (hat) on the flattened gumdrop and secure with decorating gel.

4. Slide the pretzel sticks into the middle donut, one on each side for arms.

5. Dot two eyes and a mouth on the donut hole with the decorating gel for a face.

6. Dot two buttons on the middle donut with the decorating gel.

7. Cut off the tip end of the candy corn for a nose, then carefully poke it into the donut hole. Use decorating gel if needed to hold it in place.

Snow Ice Cream

Ingredients and Supplies

Makes approximately 1 cup of ice cream

Large spoon

Measuring cup

4 cups fresh snow

Mixing bowl

½ cup heavy whipping cream

4 tablespoons granulated sugar

1 tablespoon vanilla

Spatula

Small bowl

Small spoon (shovel)

Optional: Airtight container

Directions

1. Use a large spoon to scoop up 4 cups of fresh snow and put it in the mixing bowl.

2. Add the whipping cream, sugar, and vanilla extract, and fold gently but thoroughly with the spatula. Transfer it to a small bowl and serve with a small spoon for a shovel.

3. Serve immediately, or freeze for at least 1 hour for firmer ice cream.

Optional: Place the ice cream in an airtight container, and pack it into a snow pile to freeze. Don't forget it's there!

Snow, Snowmen, and Snowflakes

129

Edible Snowman Poop

Ingredients and Supplies

Makes one puzzle

Twenty-four mini marshmallows

Zippered sandwich bag

Black permanent marker

1½ x 6½-inch white card stock

Red or green permanent marker

Stapler

Optional: Snowman sticker or computer

Directions

1. Put the marshmallows in the sandwich bag. Zip closed and set aside.

2. Draw a snowman with the black permanent marker on the left side of the card stock.

3. Write the following verse with the red or green permanent marker to the right of the snowman:

Here's the scoop,

Have you been naughty, not very nice?

If this is true,

Snowman Poop's my gift to you!

4. Staple the card stock over the top of the bag. All ages enjoy this Christmas gag gift.

Optional: Use a snowman sticker in place of drawing one, or you can make the label with a computer, using a snowman graphic and typing the verse.

Build an Edible Snowman

Ingredients and Supplies

Makes one

Three large
marshmallows

Two pretzel sticks

Large black gumdrop

Chocolate covered
graham cracker

Candy corn

Two chocolate chips

Three mini-chocolate
chips

Zippered sandwich bag

4 x 6-inch white
card stock

Red permanent
marker

Stapler

Optional: Computer

Directions

1. Put all the food items into the sandwich bag and zip closed.

2. Fold the card stock in half widthwise, and write the following poem on
   the outside with the red permanent marker:

   I am puzzled

   I have fallen upside down

   Do I belong in China Town?

   Put me together

   I belong in the weather

   WHAT AM I?

3. Staple the card over the top of the bag.
   If you want, write the recipient's name
   or "A Puzzle for You" on the front of
   the card.

Optional: Type the poem on a computer and
print it on card stock.

I am puzzled

I have fallen upside down

Do I belong in China Town?

Put me together

I belong in the weather

WHAT AM I?

Marshmallow Snowman

Ingredients and Supplies

Makes one snowman

Three large
marshmallows
(soft)

Toothpick

Sharp-tipped knife

Black decorating gel

Orange gumdrop

Pretzel stick

Three chocolate chips

Chocolate sandwich
cookie

Large black gumdrop

Directions

1. Stack the three marshmallows on top of each other.

2. Push the toothpick down the center of all the marshmallows to hold the snowman together.

3. Carve out two eye openings in the top marshmallow (head) with the knife, then fill them with decorating gel.

4. Cut ¼ inch off the bottom of the orange gumdrop, then cut the bottom section into six pie-shaped pieces.

5. Stick one orange piece below the eyes for the nose. You can eat the rest of the orange pieces or use them for other snowmen.

6. Squeeze five small dots of decorating gel under the nose for the mouth.

7. Break the pretzel stick in half and stick one end in each side of the middle marshmallow (body) for arms.

8. Press three chocolate chips in the body for buttons.

9. Pull the chocolate sandwich cookie apart, careful not to break it. Squirt some decorating gel on the inside of the cookie part with little or no filling, then press it gel side down on top the head for a hat brim.

10. Squirt some decorating gel on the bottom of the black gumdrop and stick it on top of the cookie to finish the snowman's hat.

Have you ever noticed that most icicles are on the south side of your house instead of the north? The sun melts snow just enough during the day that it begins to drip off the roof before freezing at night.

Yummy Flake

Ingredients and Supplies

Makes one

Zippered sandwich bag

Wrapped peppermint
candies

4 x 6-inch white
card stock

Scissors

Red permanent marker

Green permanent
marker

Stapler

Optional: Computer,
red or green paper,
and glue

Direction

1. Put the peppermint candies into the sandwich bag and zip closed.

2. Fold the card stock in half widthwise.

3. Trace the snowflake face (pattern piece #1) with the red permanent marker onto the left side of the card stock.

4. Use the red permanent marker and copy the following saying on the card stock next to the snowflake:

   You're a FLAKE, but "MINT" to say,
   Have a yummy Christmas day.

5. Line the snowflake's eyes with the green permanent marker, and create a green border at the edge of the card stock.

6. Staple the card over the top of the bag of candy.

Optional: Type and print the saying with a computer, using red or green paper, then cut to fit and glue it on the card stock. Trace the snowflake face onto the paper.

#1

Ingredients and Supplies for Snow, Snowmen, and Snowflakes

Snowman Donut

Powdered donut hole
Powdered bite-size donut
Powdered large donut
Knife
Two large black gumdrops
Black decorating gel
Two pretzel sticks
Candy corn

Snow Ice Cream

Large spoon
Measuring cup
4 cups fresh snow
Mixing bowl
½ cup heavy whipping cream
4 tablespoons granulated sugar
1 tablespoon vanilla
Spatula
Small bowl
Small spoon (shovel)
Optional: Airtight container

Edible Snowman Poop

Twenty-four mini marshmallows
Zippered sandwich bag
Black permanent marker
1½ x 6½-inch white card stock
Red or green permanent marker
Stapler
Optional: Snowman sticker or computer

Build an Edible Snowman

Three large marshmallows
Two pretzel sticks
Large black gumdrop
Chocolate covered graham cracker
Candy corn
Two chocolate chips
Three mini-chocolate chips
Zippered sandwich bag
4 x 6-inch white card stock
Red permanent marker
Stapler
Optional: Computer

Marshmallow Snowman

Three large marshmallows (soft)
Toothpick
Sharp-tipped knife
Black decorating gel
Orange gumdrop
Pretzel stick
Three chocolate chips
Chocolate sandwich cookie
Large black gumdrop

Yummy Flake

Zippered sandwich bag
Wrapped peppermint candies
4 x 6-inch white card stock
Scissors
Red permanent marker
Green permanent marker
Stapler
Optional: Computer, red or green paper, and glue

Don't forget the camera and film

A Healthy Elf

Ingredients and Supplies

			Dish
Makes one elf	Knife	Red apple	Peanut butter
			Two raisins

Directions

1. Cut off a ¼-inch round slice of the apple and lay it on the dish.

2. Scrape out areas of the apple slice with the knife for the eyes, nose, and mouth.

3. Fill those areas with peanut butter.

4. Put the raisins on top of the peanut butter eyes.

5. Carve out another section of the apple in the shape of a Santa hat; attach it to the top of the elf's face with peanut butter, being sure to keep the skin side up.

6. Cut a small round piece of apple and attach it to the tip of the Santa hat with peanut butter.

7. Carve out a small section from each side of the face to place the ears.

8. Cut elf ears out of another section of the apple and attach to the sides of the face using peanut butter. Serve immediately before it browns.

Elves' Favorite Candy Train

Ingredients and Supplies

		Four wrapped peppermints
Makes one train	Roll of Lifesavers®	One Hershey's Kiss®
Glue gun	Pack of chewing gum (five sticks)	1½ x ½-inch box of of Christmas candy

Directions

1. Glue the roll of Lifesavers® parallel to and on top of the chewing gum.

2. Glue the four mints onto the chewing gum, two on each side, to represent wheels.

3. Glue the Hershey's Kiss® on top of the roll of Lifesavers® toward one end for a smokestack.

4. Glue the box of candy lengthwise on top of the roll of Lifesavers® behind the smokestack. Have a "treatful" ride!

Santa's Candy Sleigh

Ingredients and Supplies

Makes one sleigh

Royal Icing (ingredients and recipe below)

Decorating bag

Decorating coupler

Decorating tip #3

Three graham crackers (each is four sections)

Two candy canes (unwrapped)

Chocolate foil-covered Santa (approximately 4 inches tall)

Assorted Christmas candy

Variation: Glue gun

Royal Icing

Wilton® Meringue Powder

Powdered sugar

Water

Mixer and bowl

Spoon or spatula

Directions

1. Follow the directions on the can of meringue powder mix to make a recipe of Royal Icing.

2. Working quickly, put the Royal Icing into the decorating bag, coupler and tip already in place.

3. Squeeze the icing on top of one graham cracker, then quickly place another graham cracker on top.

4. Squeeze the icing onto both candy canes and attach one on each side of the long edges of the crackers.

5. Carefully break the third graham cracker in half widthwise.

6. Again working quickly, attach half of the graham cracker standing on its edge on the back of the sleigh. (The front has the curved portion of the candy canes.)

7. Carefully break apart the last half of the third graham cracker.

8. Quickly attach one half on each side, long edges on top of the candy canes and short edges touching the back of the sleigh.

9. Let the sleigh sit for a few hours to harden.

10. Fill the sleigh with the chocolate Santa Claus and assorted Christmas candy.

11. This is an edible sleigh. Simply pull the crackers and candy canes apart to eat Santa and his sleigh!

Note: You will have plenty of Royal Icing to make more sleighs.

Variation: You can use a glue gun to glue the sleigh together, but it will not be edible.

Santa's Chocolate Sleigh Bell Cookies

Ingredients and Supplies

Makes 3 to 4 dozen cookies

½ cup butter

2 cups peanut butter

Saucepan

Spoon or spatula

Large bowl

3½ cups powdered sugar

3½ cups Kellogg's™ Rice Krispies® Cereal

Three cookie sheets

Wax paper

12-ounce bag semi-sweet chocolate chips

3 ounces chocolate candy bars

One-third bar paraffin wax

Double boiler

Toothpicks

Directions

1. Melt the butter and peanut butter in the saucepan on low-medium heat, stirring constantly.

2. In the large bowl, stir the powdered sugar and cereal together.

3. Line the cookie sheets with wax paper.

4. Pour the peanut butter mixture into the cereal mixture, and mix thoroughly.

5. With clean hands, roll the mixture into 1-inch balls and place them on the cookie sheets.

6. Put the cookie sheets in the refrigerator while you melt the chocolate.

7. Put the chocolate chips, candy bars, and paraffin wax in the double boiler, with water in the bottom, and let them all melt, stirring occasionally.

8. Poke each cookie ball with a toothpick, then dip into the chocolate mixture. Hold the cookie over the double boiler for a few seconds to let any excess chocolate drip off. Shake the cookie slightly over the cookie sheet to let it fall off the toothpick.

9. Fill any toothpick hole with a drop of chocolate if needed.

10. It's not necessary to refrigerate the cookies, but they're delicious when cold.

Tip: Don't use oily peanut butter because the cookies won't roll properly.

Tell us about your most memorable Christmas party?

"Our annual Christmas Cookie Exchange was always the kickoff to the holiday season and greatly anticipated by all who attended. The house was filled with laughter of renewed acquaintances and the excitement of Christmas. Of course, tasting new cookies made from the recipes submitted was essential. Our cookie party, designated one of the best things to do in Colorado during the holidays, was so successful that people asked to be included in a guest list that was already at seventy-five. Since it led to the creation of our first cookbook, Colorado Cookie Collection, new careers in publishing, and an opportunity to work with each other, our Christmas Cookie Exchange will always hold fond memories. To this day, we have friends tell us they miss the cookie exchange; maybe one of these seasons, we will host a 'reunion' one."

—Cyndi Duncan and Georgie Patrick Authors of *Nothin' but Muffins, Cookie Exchange,* and a new "quick" series including their latest, *Quick Hors d'oeuvres*

Elf Tool Cookies

Ingredients and Supplies

Makes 15 large or 24 small cookies

2¾ tablespoons shortening

½ cup brown sugar (packed firmly)

¾ cup dark molasses

⅓ cup water

Mixer and bowl

Spoon or spatula

3½ cups flour

½ teaspoon salt

1 teaspoon baking soda

½ teaspoon ground allspice

½ teaspoon ground cloves

½ teaspoon cinnamon

1 teaspoon ground ginger

Medium bowl

Plastic wrap

Rolling pin

Tool-shaped cookie cutters

Greased cookie sheets

Glaze (ingredients and recipe below)

Decorating bag

Decorating coupler

Decorating tip #3 or #4

Wax paper

Small toolbox (found at hardware stores)

Excelsior (wood shavings)

Colored pencils or markers

3 x 5-inch card stock

Paper hole puncher

6 inches Christmas ribbon

Variation: Computer

Glaze

Mixer and bowl

1 cup powdered sugar

1 tablespoon milk

1 tablespoon vanilla

Food coloring (any color)

Spoon or spatula

What do you eat for Christmas?

"Sugar cereals are a special treat for my children. I stress a nutritious breakfast and tend to avoid candied cereals. On Christmas morning, however, they are delighted to discover Santa breaking Mom's rules and leaving them a box of Christmas CAP'N CRUNCH® under the tree!"

—Renee Zumpano
Akron, Ohio

Directions

1. Cream the shortening, brown sugar, molasses, and water together in mixer bowl.

2. Put the flour, salt, baking soda, allspice, cloves, cinnamon, and ginger together in a medium bowl and stir.

3. Mix the flour mixture into the shortening mixture.

4. Cover the dough with plastic wrap and put in the refrigerator for 2 hours.

5. Preheat oven to 350°.

6. Roll the dough ¼ inch thick on a lightly floured counter. (It also helps to flour the rolling pin.)

7. Cut with the tool-shaped cookie cutters (floured) and bake on greased cookie sheets for 10 to 12 minutes or until you get no mark when you touch a cookie. Let cool.

8. Spread glaze on top of each cookie. If you would like a tool-shaped outline on the cookies put leftover glaze into the decorating bag, with the coupler and tip already in place, and "outline" the cookies.

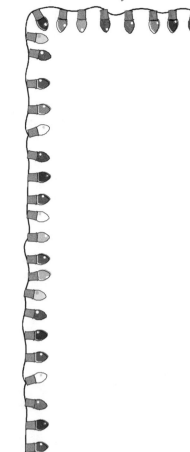

9. Lay the cookies on wax paper and let them sit a few hours to harden.

10. Line the toolbox with excelsior and fill them with cookies.

11. Draw and color an elf on the card stock or trace the elf illustration found on page 99. Write "Elf Tools" next to the elf.

12. Punch a hole into the corner of the card stock, slide the ribbon through the card stock, and tie to the toolbox handle.

Note: You can use this recipe to make other Christmas-shaped cookies such as gingerbread people.

Variation: Make the "Elf Tools" label with a computer, using an elf graphic and some elf-like font.

Glaze Directions

1. Blend the powdered sugar, milk, and vanilla in the small bowl.

2. Stir in 2 to 3 drops of food coloring.

3. If the glaze seems too thick, add ½ tablespoon of milk, one at a time, being careful not to thin the glaze too much.

Note: To make different colors of glaze, put the glaze into several bowls, stir a different food coloring into each bowl, and use a new decorating bag, coupler, and tip for each color.

Santa's Chimneys

What do you think? Santa needs to get down the chimney, set out the gifts, and climb out of the chimney in a minute or less. **Can he do it?**

Ingredients and Supplies

Makes one chimney

Chocolate graham cracker

1-inch cube frozen pound cake

Butter knife

12-ounce can white frosting

3-inch square cardboard

Two tubes red decorating gel

Edible silver glitter (found at craft stores)

Medium-size chocolate foil-covered Santa

Bag of cotton candy

Optional: Bar cookie recipe

Directions

1. Carefully break the graham cracker into four pieces. Make the chimney by arranging the four pieces, standing on end, around the 1-inch cube of frozen pound cake. If needed, trim the pound cake to fit.

2. "Glue" the graham crackers to the pound cake with the frosting and knife.

3. "Glue" the chimney onto the center of the cardboard.

4. Using the red decorating gel, draw bricks on the chimney. Let dry.

5. Spread a layer of frosting onto the cardboard around the chimney to represent snow. Sprinkle edible glitter on top of the snow.

6. Place the chocolate Santa inside the chimney.

7. Put some cotton candy inside the chimney and around Santa for smoke.

Optional: Instead of the pound cake, use any bar cookie recipe. Just cut a section after baked to fit inside the graham crackers.

A Healthy Elf

Knife
Red apple
Dish
Peanut butter
Two raisins

Elves' Favorite Candy Train

Glue gun
Roll of Lifesavers®
Pack of chewing gum
  (five sticks)
Four wrapped
  peppermints
One Hershey's Kiss®
1½ x ½-inch box of
  Christmas candy

Santa's Candy Sleigh

Royal Icing (ingredients
  in next column to right)
Decorating bag
Decorating coupler
Decorating tip #3
Three graham crackers
  (each is four sections)
Two candy canes
  (unwrapped)
Chocolate foil-covered
  Santa (approximately
  4 inches tall)
Assorted Christmas
  candy
Variation: Glue gun
  (continued)

Royal Icing

Wilton® Meringue Powder
Powdered sugar
Water
Mixer and bowl
Spoon or spatula

Santa's Chocolate Sleigh Bell Cookies

½ cup butter
2 cups peanut butter
Saucepan
Spoon or spatula
Large bowl
3½ cups powdered sugar
3½ cups Kellogg's™
  Rice Krispies® Cereal
Three cookie sheets
Wax paper
12-ounce bag semi-
  sweet chocolate chips
3 ounces chocolate
  candy bars
One-third bar paraffin wax
Double boiler
Toothpicks

Elf Tool Cookies

2¾ tablespoons
  shortening
½ cup brown sugar
  (packed firmly)
  (continued)

¾ cup dark molasses
⅓ cup water
Mixer and bowl
Spoon or spatula
3½ cups flour
½ teaspoon salt
1 teaspoon baking soda
½ teaspoon ground
  allspice
½ teaspoon ground
  cloves
½ teaspoon cinnamon
1 teaspoon ground ginger
Medium bowl
Plastic wrap
Rolling pin
Tool-shaped cookie
  cutters
Greased cookie sheets
Glaze (ingredients in
  next column to right)
Decorating bag
Decorating coupler
Decorating tip #3 or #4
Wax paper
Small toolbox (found
  at hardware stores)
Excelsior (wood shavings)
Colored pencils or
  markers
3 x 5-inch card stock
Paper hole puncher
6 inches Christmas
  ribbon
Variation: Computer
  (continued)

Ingredients and Supplies for Santa and His Elves

Glaze

Mixer and bowl
1 cup powdered sugar
1 tablespoon milk
1 tablespoon vanilla
Food coloring (any color)
Spoon or spatula

Santa's Chimneys

Chocolate graham
  cracker
1-inch cube frozen
  pound cake
Butter knife
12-ounce can white
  frosting
3-inch square cardboard
Two tubes red
  decorating gel
Edible silver glitter
  (found at craft stores)
Medium-size chocolate
  foil-covered Santa
Bag of cotton candy
Optional: Bar cookie
  recipe

141

Reindeer Droppings

Ingredients and Supplies

Makes one

Pencil

6 x 8-inch brown craft foam

Scissors

Glue gun

3.4-ounce "milk carton" Whoppers®

2-inch tan pom-pom

1-inch tan pom-pom

¼-inch red pom-pom

Two 12mm moving eyes

¾ x 10-inch brown vinyl

Card stock

Red permanent marker

Paper hole puncher

Three ¾-inch red jingle bells

18 inches 1mm leather cord

Optional: Computer

Directions

1. Trace two reindeer antlers (pattern piece #1, page 143) onto the brown craft foam and cut out.

2. Glue the antlers to one side of the carton at the top.

3. Glue the 2-inch tan pom-pom (reindeer face) over the bottom of the antlers.

4. Glue the 1-inch tan pom-pom on top of it ("snout") and the red pom-pom (nose) on top of that.

5. Glue the moving eyes onto the face above the snout.

6. Wrap and glue the brown vinyl under the face around the carton.

7. Write the following on the card stock:

> *Santa is coming*
> *Led by reindeer;*
> *For you they bring*
> *A yummy reindeer treat—*
> *Reindeer droppings*
> *Good enough to eat!*

8. Punch a hole in the corner of the card stock.

9. Slide the three jingle bells onto the leather cording.

10. Glue the leather cording onto the brown vinyl under the face and around the sides of the carton for reindeer reins. Be sure to space the bells evenly, and leave the reins free in back and equal in length.

11. Slide the card stock onto one rein and tie the reins together at their ends.

Optional: Use a computer to print out the verse on a card.

Santa is coming
Led by reindeer;
For you they bring
A yummy reindeer treat-
Reindeer droppings
Good enough to eat!

Rudolph and His Reindeer

Reindeer Droppings pattern

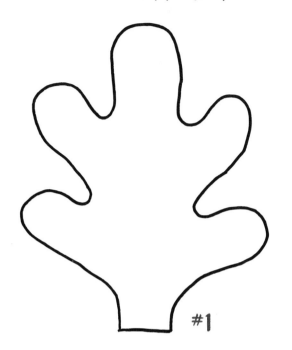

#1

Reindeer or Rudolph Noses

Ingredients and Supplies

Make as much as you want for a party

Any of the following in a bowl or bowls:
  Maraschino cherries
  Cherry tomatoes

Raspberries
Cinnamon imperials
Red gumdrops, gumballs, M&M's®, Skittles®, or jelly beans

White blank index card
Red permanent marker

Directions

1. Put one of the red food items in a bowl or put several in separate bowls.

2. Bend about one-third of the index card widthwise so it will stand on its own. Use the red permanent marker to write "Reindeer Noses" or "Rudolph Noses" on the card just above the bend, as shown in illustration.

3. Stand the card up near the bowl.

Rudolph Noses

Standing Candy Reindeer

Ingredients and Supplies

Makes one reindeer

Two large white gumdrops

Four pretzel sticks

Two miniature chocolate chips

Cinnamon imperial

Directions

1. Roll one gumdrop in your hand to make a long, thick roll for a reindeer body.

2. Break all the pretzel sticks in half.

3. Stick one pretzel half in the flat side of the second gumdrop (head), then attach it to one end of the rolled gumdrop (body).

4. Push four pretzel halves into the underside of the body, two in the front and two in the back for legs.

5. Put two pretzel halves in the top of the head for antlers. Eat the last pretzel half!

6. Push the two chocolate chips into the head for eyes, and then the cinnamon imperial for a nose.

7. Stand the reindeer on its legs, adjusting them if needed.

Reindeer Sandwich

Ingredients and Supplies

Makes one sandwich

Butter knife

Peanut butter

Two slices bread

Pretzel sticks

Two black jellybeans

Maraschino cherry

Variation: Celery or carrots, lunchmeat or cream cheese/chives spread, cherry tomato, and/or soft tortilla

Directions

1. Spread your peanut butter between the bread slices.

2. Cut the sandwich into a large triangle, trimming off all the crust.

3. Stick pretzels in two corners so they stick out like antlers.

4. Squish the black jellybeans into the sandwich below the pretzels for eyes, and the maraschino cherry at the third corner of the sandwich for the reindeer nose.

Variation: Replace any of the ingredients with the following choices depending on people's taste:

Instead of pretzel sticks, use celery or carrots, thinly sliced.

Instead of peanut butter, use lunchmeat or cream cheese/chives spread.

Instead of a maraschino cherry, use a cherry tomato.

Instead of bread, use a soft tortilla.

Bagged Reindeer Oatmeal Food

Ingredients and Supplies

Makes 4 bags

⅓ cup butter

Saucepan

½ cup brown sugar

¼ teaspoon baking soda

Spoon or spatula

1½ cups oatmeal

Greased 8-inch square pan

Knife

Paper towels

Pencil

12 x 18-inch brown craft foam

Scissors

Four brown paper lunch bags

Glue gun

Four 1½-inch red pom-poms

Eight 20mm moving eyes

Variation: Store-bought crunchy oatmeal granola bars

Directions

1. Melt the butter in the saucepan over low heat.

2. Turn the heat to medium-high and add the brown sugar and baking soda. Mix well.

3. When the mixture is foamy, stir in the oatmeal.

4. Dump the oatmeal mixture into the greased pan and bake at 350° for 8 to 10 minutes or until lightly brown.

5. While hot, cut the oatmeal into four bars.

6. Wait about 10 minutes, then take each bar out of the pan and lay it on a paper towel to absorb any excess oil. Don't worry if it crumbles—the reindeer like it that way.

7. Trace eight reindeer antlers (pattern piece #1, page 143) onto the brown craft foam and cut out.

8. Put a bar of the oatmeal mixture into each lunch bag.

9. Fold the top right and left corners of each lunch bag down to form a point at the top of the bag. Then fold that section down and glue a pom-pom (reindeer nose) at the point, which is now facing down.

10. Glue two moving eyes above each nose.

11. Glue two antlers onto the top back of each bag so they're sticking up.

12. Eat the reindeer oatmeal on Christmas Eve, but save some to sprinkle on the lawn for Rudolph and his friends!

Variation: Purchase store-bought crunchy oatmeal granola bars and use them instead of making the granola recipe.

Note: Chances are animals will eat the food you sprinkle outside, but the oatmeal granola won't hurt them.

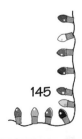

Reindeer Cookies

Ingredients and Supplies

Makes 24 cookies

Mixer and bowl

Spoon or spatula

½ cup shortening

¼ cup butter

Two eggs

1 cup sugar

1 teaspoon vanilla

2½ cups all-purpose flour

¼ teaspoon salt

1 teaspoon baking powder

Small bowl

Tablespoon

Cookie sheets

Forty-eight brown M&M's®

Twenty-four red M&M's®

Forty-eight mini pretzels

Optional: Rolling pin, flour, and triangular-shaped cookie cutter

Directions

1. Cream the shortening, butter, eggs, sugar, and vanilla together.

2. Put the flour, salt, and baking powder together in a small bowl and stir.

3. Blend the flour mixture into the shortening mixture.

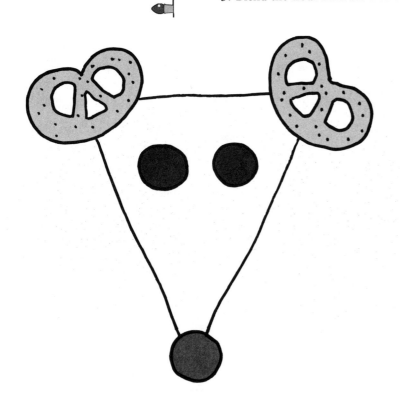

4. Refrigerate the dough for 1 hour.

5. Pre-heat oven to 400°.

6. Take tablespoon-size pieces of dough, form them into triangles, and place them onto ungreased cookie sheets a couple of inches apart.

7. For each cookie, add two brown M&M's® for reindeer eyes, a red M&M® for the nose, and two pretzels for antlers.

8. Bake about 6 to 8 minutes or until lightly brown. Cool.

Optional: Roll the dough ⅛ inch thick on a lightly floured counter and cut with the triangular-shaped cookie cutter.

Reindeer Droppings

Pencil
6 x 8-inch brown
   craft foam
Scissors
Glue gun
3.4-ounce "milk carton"
   Whoppers®
2-inch tan pom-pom
1-inch tan pom-pom
¼-inch red pom-pom
Two 12mm moving eyes
¾ x 10-inch brown vinyl
Card stock
Red permanent marker
Paper hole puncher
Three ¾-inch red
   jingle bells
18 inches 1mm
   leather cord
Optional: Computer

Reindeer or Rudolph Noses

Any of the following
in a bowl or bowls:
   Maraschino cherries
   Cherry tomatoes
   Raspberries
   Cinnamon imperials
   Red gumdrops,
      gumballs, M&M's®,
      Skittles®, or jelly
      beans
White blank index card
Red permanent marker

Standing Candy Reindeer

Two large white
   gumdrops
Four pretzel sticks
Two miniature
   chocolate chips
Cinnamon imperial

Reindeer Sandwich

Butter knife
Peanut butter
Two slices bread
Pretzel sticks
Two black jellybeans
Maraschino cherry
Variation: Celery or
   carrots, lunchmeat or
   cream cheese/chives
   spread, cherry tomato,
   and/or soft tortilla

Don't forget the
camera and film

Bagged Reindeer Oatmeal Food

⅛ cup butter
Saucepan
½ cup brown sugar
¼ teaspoon baking soda
Spoon or spatula
1½ cups oatmeal
Greased 8-inch
   square pan
Knife
Paper towels
Pencil
12 x 18-inch brown
   craft foam
Scissors
Four brown paper
   lunch bags
Glue gun
Four 1½-inch red
   pom-poms
Eight 20mm moving eyes
Variation: Store-bought
   crunchy oatmeal
   granola bars

Ingredients and Supplies for Rudolph and His Reindeer

Reindeer Cookies

Mixer and bowl
Spoon or spatula
½ cup shortening
¼ cup butter
Two eggs
1 cup sugar
1 teaspoon vanilla
2½ cups all-purpose
   flour
¼ teaspoon salt
1 teaspoon baking powder
Small bowl
Tablespoon
Cookie sheets
Forty-eight brown M&M's®
Twenty-four red M&M's®
Forty-eight mini pretzels
Optional: Rolling pin,
   flour, and triangular-
   shaped cookie
   cutter

Edible Candy Angel

Ingredients and Supplies

Makes one	Small plate	Creme Bite
Two Hershey's Kisses® (silver)	Royal Icing (ingredients and recipe below)	Strawberry Fruit by the Foot®
Knife	Hershey's® Cookies 'n'	Decorating Décors red sugar crystals
Potato peeler		*Optional:* Small white gumball
Royal Icing	Powdered sugar	Mixer and bowl
Wilton® Meringue Powder	Water	Spoon or spatula

Directions

1. Pull out the paper message from one of the Hershey's Kisses®. Discard.

2. Cut the tip, foil and all, off the Hershey's Kiss®. Be sure to leave the foil on the bottom part. Set aside.

3. Unwrap the other kiss and with the potato peeler, shred the chocolate into the small plate. Set aside.

4. Follow the directions on the Wilton® Meringue powder to make the Royal Icing.

5. With the knife, dab a drop of meringue onto the cut part of the Hershey's Kiss® (the angel's body). Quickly place the Hershey's® Cookies 'n' Creme Bite on top for the angel's head.

6. Spread some icing on the "scalp" of the head, then quickly roll it in the shredded chocolate to give the angel hair. Set aside.

7. Roll out the Fruit by the Foot® and cut a ¼ x 2 inch section for the wings. Slice that section into two ¼ x 1-inch pieces and stack them on top of each other, pressing them together.

8. Using the knife, fringe both ends of the Fruit by the Foot®, leaving a middle section intact. Dab some Royal Icing onto the middle section of the wings and stick the wings behind the angel's body.

9. Cut another section of the Fruit by the Foot®, ⅛ x 2½ inches. Spread a thin layer of Royal Icing on one side and immediately shake sugar crystals on it. Wait a few minutes for the sugar to stick, then bend and squeeze the ends together to form an angel's halo. Set it on top of the angel's head.

10. Let the angel sit for a few hours to harden.

11. This is an edible angel. The children can eat all the candy after taking the foil off the Hershey's Kiss®.

Note: You will have plenty of icing left over to make lots of angels.

Optional: A small white gumball can work for the head as well.

I Believe in Angels

Singing Angel Cupcake

Ingredients and Supplies

Makes 24 to 28 cupcakes

Cake mix (any flavor)

Christmas cupcake liners

Cupcake baking tin

16-ounce can pink or white frosting

Gold foil-covered chocolate coins (one per cupcake)

Four tubes black decorating gel

Four tubes red decorating gel

Bag of wavy potato chips

Knife

Directions

1. Bake the cupcakes using the directions on the box and let cool.

2. Frost all the cupcakes.

3. Use the red decorating gel to draw angel hair on each cupcake (angel's face).

4. Use the black decorating gel to draw angel eyes and a singing mouth on each cupcake.

5. Insert a gold coin into the side of each cupcake above the hair.

6. Insert a potato chip into each cupcake on either side of the hair for angel wings.

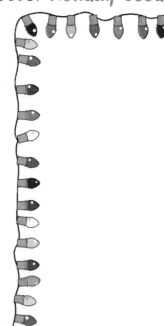

Angel Clouds

Ingredients and Supplies

Makes 2 clouds

Bag of cotton candy (found at grocery or video stores)

Two plates

Optional: Edible glitter (found at craft stores)

Directions

1. This is simple. Pull the cotton candy apart, careful not to squish it.

2. Lay it on the plates and serve.

Optional: Add some edible glitter on top for pizzazz.

149

Create-an-Angel

Ingredients and Supplies

Makes approximately 8 angels

Angel food cake

Marshmallows (small and large)

Toothpicks

Directions

1. Spread all the items on a table.

2. Let each person create an angel using any of the items.

3. Before anyone eats his angel, have him spend 1 minute telling the others how his angel got its wings.

4. Remind them to remove all the toothpicks before eating.

Sparkling Angel Clouds and Stars

Ingredients and Supplies

Makes one dessert

Ready-made blue Jell-O® gelatin (snack-size)

Canned whipped cream

Yellow edible glitter (found at craft or kitchen stores)

Decorating Décors candy stars

Directions

1. Peel off the foil lid of the gelatin snack.

2. Squirt a pile of whipped cream (clouds) on top of the gelatin.

3. Sprinkle the edible glitter on the whipped cream.

4. Scatter some stars on top of everything.

Creamy Angel Caramel Dip

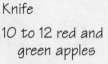

Ingredients and Supplies

Makes 4½ cups caramel dip

½ cup butter

Electric fondue pot

2 cups brown sugar

2 tablespoons water

14-ounce can sweetened condensed milk

¾ cup corn syrup

Spatula or spoon

Knife

10 to 12 red and green apples

1 teaspoon vanilla

Optional: Plastic container with lid, and microwave

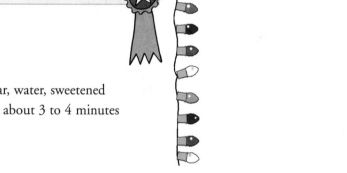

Directions

1. Melt the butter in the fondue pot on low.

2. Turn up the heat to medium and add the brown sugar, water, sweetened condensed milk, and corn syrup. Stir to blend. Cook about 3 to 4 minutes until creamy, stirring occasionally.

3. Slice the apples and set aside.

4. Turn heat to low, add vanilla, and mix well. Serve with the apple slices.

Optional: Save any excess dip in a plastic container and reheat in microwave.

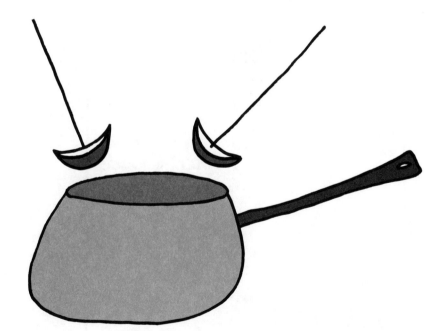

Ingredients and Supplies for I Believe in Angels

Edible Candy Angel

Two Hershey's
  Kisses® (silver)
Knife
Potato peeler
Small plate
Royal Icing
  (ingredients below)
Hershey's® Cookies 'n'
  Creme Bite
Strawberry Fruit
  by the Foot®
Decorating Décors
  red sugar crystals
Optional: Small white
  gumball

Royal Icing
Wilton® Meringue
  Powder
Powdered sugar
Water
Mixer and bowl
Spoon or spatula

Don't forget the
camera and film

Singing Angel Cupcake

Cake mix (any flavor)
Christmas cupcake
  liners
Cupcake baking tin
16-ounce can pink
  or white frosting
Gold foil-covered
  chocolate coins (one
  per cupcake)
Four tubes black
  decorating gel
Four tubes red
  decorating gel
Bag of wavy potato chips
Knife

Angel Clouds

Bag of cotton candy
  (found at grocery
  or video stores)
Two plates
Optional: Edible glitter
  (found at craft stores)

Create-an-Angel

Angel food cake
Marshmallows
  (small and large)
Toothpicks

Sparkling Angel Clouds and Stars

Ready-made blue
  Jell-O® gelatin
  (snack-size)
Canned whipped cream
Yellow edible glitter
  (found at craft or
  kitchen stores)
Decorating Décors
  candy stars

Creamy Angel Caramel Dip

½ cup butter
Electric fondue pot
2 cups brown sugar
2 tablespoons water
14-ounce can sweetened
  condensed milk
¾ cup corn syrup
Spatula or spoon
Knife
10 to 12 red and
  green apples
1 teaspoon vanilla
Optional: Plastic
  container with lid, and
  microwave

King Cake
France

Ingredients and Supplies

Makes 2 cakes

Cake mix (any flavor)

Mixer and bowl

Spoon or spatula

Two round 10-inch cake pans

Two dried beans (any kind)

Two serving plates

16-ounce can frosting (any color)

Icing spatula or knife

Directions

1. Make two single-layer cakes, following the directions on the box for two 10-inch round pans, except put a bean in each pan before baking. Let the cakes cool, then flip each onto a serving plate.

2. Spread the frosting on the top and sides of each cake.

3. Cut and serve the cake. Whoever has a bean inside his slice is "King" for a day. Tradition calls for children to hand out the slices.

Caution: Explain to those eating that there could be a bean in their piece and to be careful not to swallow it.

Optional: Make one cake a King Cake and the other a Queen Cake. Males eat the King Cake, and females eat the Queen Cake. One lady will be "Queen" for the day. One male will be "King" for the day.

Christmas Here, There, and Everywhere—Global Celebrations

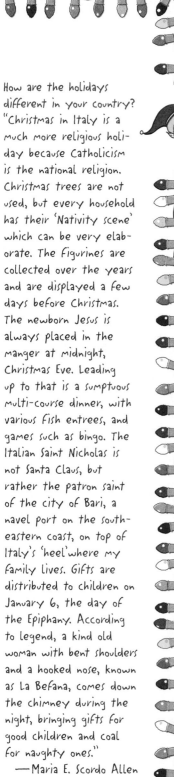

Fried Cheese
Sicily, Italy

How are the holidays different in your country? "Christmas in Italy is a much more religious holiday because Catholicism is the national religion. Christmas trees are not used, but every household has their 'Nativity scene' which can be very elaborate. The figurines are collected over the years and are displayed a few days before Christmas. The newborn Jesus is always placed in the manger at midnight, Christmas Eve. Leading up to that is a sumptuous multi-course dinner, with various fish entrees, and games such as bingo. The Italian Saint Nicholas is not Santa Claus, but rather the patron saint of the city of Bari, a navel port on the southeastern coast, on top of Italy's 'heel' where my family lives. Gifts are distributed to children on January 6, the day of the Epiphany. According to legend, a kind old woman with bent shoulders and a hooked nose, known as La Befana, comes down the chimney during the night, bringing gifts for good children and coal for naughty ones."
—Maria E. Scordo Allen
Honorary Vice Consul
of Italy
Littleton, Colorado

Ingredients and Supplies

Makes 4 to 5 servings
Knife
1 pound asiago cheese
2 tablespoons olive oil

Large sauté pan
Spatula
Clove of garlic (chopped)

2 teaspoons wine vinegar
Pinch of sugar
½ teaspoon Italian seasoning

Directions

1. Cut the cheese into ¼-inch strips.

2. Heat the olive oil in the pan, and sauté the garlic.

3. When the garlic turns brown, throw it away and lay the cheese in the pan over low heat.

4. Fry both sides.

5. First, sprinkle the vinegar over the cheese, then the sugar, and finally the Italian seasoning, on one side only.

6. Cook for about 5 more minutes. Do not let the cheese overcook as it will harden. Serve immediately.

Potato Pancakes
Germany

Ingredients and Supplies

Makes approximately
26 pancakes

Potato peeler

Seven medium
potatoes

Food processor or hand
shredder/grater

Large bowl

Medium onion

Two eggs

Large slotted spoon

2 tablespoons flour

¼ teaspoon salt

⅛ teaspoon pepper

Oil

Large frying pan

Spatula

Paper towels

Optional: Cinnamon
applesauce

Directions

1. Peel the potatoes, then shred them into the large bowl.

2. Peel and shred the onion, then add it to the potatoes.

3. Add the eggs, salt, and pepper, and mix well.

4. Sprinkle the flour over the potato mixture and mix well. The flour will
   help hold the pancakes together.

5. Heat the oil in the pan.

6. Scoop out a "pancake-size" piece of the potato mixture and fry on both
   sides until brown.

7. Lay on a paper towel to blot excess oil before serving.

8. Continue to fry pancakes,
   adding more oil if needed.

Optional: Serve with cinnamon
applesauce.

Santa Claus is called in
other countries:
Pe`re Noëls – France
Julemand – Denmark
Dun Che Lao Pen – China
Papai Noel – Brazil

Do you have any special
ornaments you look for-
ward to hanging each
year, and who gets to
hang them?
"A pickle. It's a German
tradition to hang one on
the tree secretly and
the first person to find
it gets to open the first
gift. In our family, this is
a family gift, a game or
something we can do as
a family."

—Shalaine Root
Thornton, Colorado

Candy Kinara (candelabrum)
To Celebrate Kwanzaa

Ingredients and Supplies

Makes one cracker

Seven lemon drops

One whole graham cracker

Decorating gel (any color)

Knife

Sour Punch® strawberry candy straw

Sour Punch® sour apple candy straw

Black licorice stick

Directions

1. Line the lemon drops (candle flames) equally spaced across the top of a long side of the graham cracker (candelabrum).

2. Put a dab of decorating gel under each lemon drop to hold it in place.

3. Cut the strawberry candy straw into three 1½-inch pieces and discard the rest. Do the same with the sour apple candy straw.

4. Cut a 1½-inch piece of licorice (black candle) and discard the rest. Place it under the middle lemon drop (candle flame).

5. Lay the strawberry candy straw pieces (red candles) to the left side of the licorice, one under each lemon drop.

6. Lay the sour apple candy straw pieces (green candles) to the right side of the licorice, one under each lemon drop.

7. Place a dab of decorating gel under each candle to secure them to the graham cracker kinara (candelabrum).

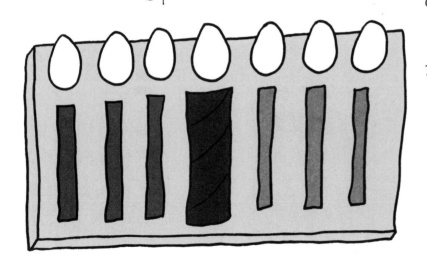

Goody-Filled Wooden Shoes
Holland

Ingredients and Supplies

Serves several

Pair of new wooden shoes
(purchase on
the Internet)

Christmas candy

Christmas cookies

Directions

1. Fill the shoes, one with candy and the other with cookies.

2. Serve as a centerpiece or on a coffee table.

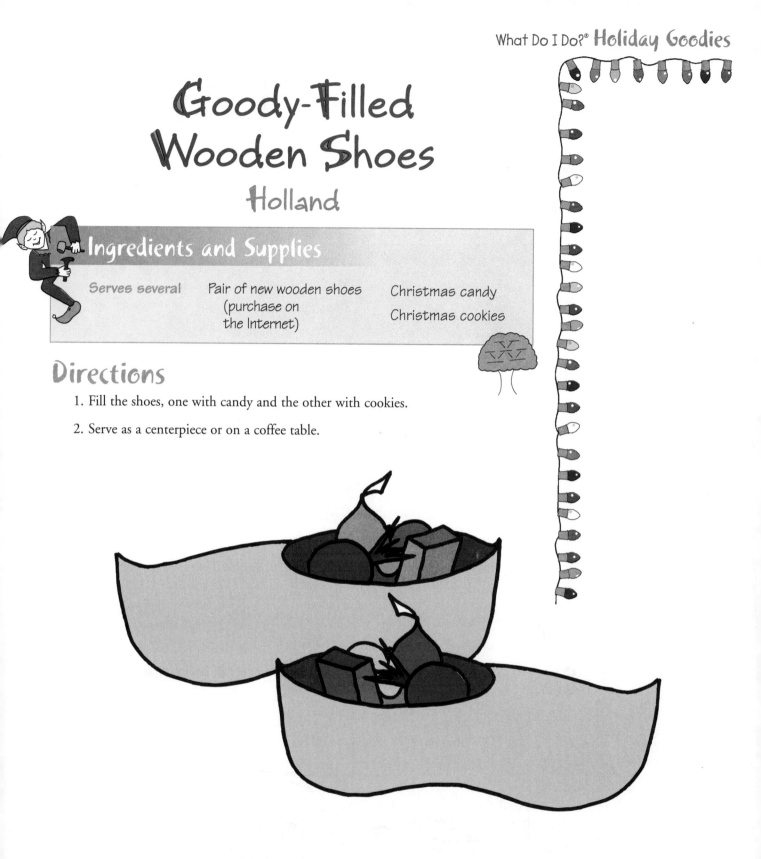

Cranberry Pudding
Russia

Ingredients and Supplies

Serves 6 to 8

1 pound cranberries

1 cup sugar

2 cups water

Saucepan

Spatula or spoon

Blender

Strainer

2 tablespoons orange juice

2 tablespoons cornstarch

Small bowl and wire whip

Optional: Canned whipped cream or heavy cream

Directions

1. Put the cranberries, sugar, and water into the saucepan.

2. Cook on low until the cranberries pop, about 12 to 15 minutes, stirring occasionally.

3. Puree the mixture in a blender.

4. To remove the cranberry seeds, push the mixture through the strainer.

5. Put the mixture back into the saucepan.

6. Pour the orange juice into the cornstarch, mix together, then stir into the saucepan.

7. Cook on low heat to thicken, stirring constantly.

8. Serve cold.

Optional: Either squirt whipped cream on top of the pudding or pour heavy cream over it.

How to say "Merry Christmas" in other countries and cultures:

Philippines Maligayang Pasko

Mexico Feliz Navidad

Denmark Glaedelig Jul

Germany Fröhliche Weihnachten

Greece Kala Christougena

France Joyeux Noël

Italy Buon Natale

Sweden God Jul

Hawaiian Mele Kalikimaka

Indonesia Selamet Hari Natal

Brazil Feliz Natal

Dutch "Vrolijk Kerstfeest"

King Cake
France

Cake mix (any flavor)
Mixer and bowl
Spoon or spatula
Two round 10-inch
  cake pans
Two dried beans
  (any kind)
Two serving plates
16-ounce can frosting
  (any color)
Icing spatula or knife

Fried Cheese
Sicily, Italy

Knife
1 pound asiago cheese
2 tablespoons olive oil
Large sauté pan
Spatula
Clove of garlic (chopped)
2 teaspoons wine
  vinegar
Pinch of sugar
½ teaspoon Italian
  seasoning

Potato Pancakes
Germany

Potato peeler
Seven medium potatoes
Food processor or hand
  shredder/grater
Large bowl
Medium onion
Two eggs
Large slotted spoon
2 tablespoons flour
¼ teaspoon salt
⅛ teaspoon pepper
Oil
Large frying pan
Spatula
Paper towels
Optional: Cinnamon
  applesauce

Don't forget the
camera and film

Candy Kinara
(candelabrum)
To Celebrate Kwanzaa

Seven lemon drops
One whole graham
  cracker
Decorating gel
  (any color)
Knife
Sour Punch® strawberry
  candy straw
Sour Punch® sour
  apple candy straw
Black licorice stick

Goody-Filled Wooden Shoes
Holland

Pair of new wooden
  shoes (purchase
  on the Internet)
Christmas candy
Christmas cookies

Ingredients and Supplies for Christmas Here, There, and Everywhere—Glocal Celebrations

Cranberry Pudding
Russia

1 pound cranberries
1 cup sugar
2 cups water
Saucepan
Spatula or spoon
Blender
Strainer
2 tablespoons
  orange juice
2 tablespoons
  cornstarch
Small bowl and
  wire whip
Optional: Canned
  whipped cream
  or heavy cream

CHAPTER 5

Drinks

Helpful Hints for Drinks

1. Check your recipe to see if there are any preparations to do ahead of time.

2. Freeze fresh snow in freezer bags to use at a later date.

3. Use red or green plastic cups, or both, for a holiday look.

4. Cut star shapes out of lime peelings and float them on top of drinks.

5. Garnish a drink with a maraschino cherry wrapped in green lime peeling and secured with a toothpick, but first lay the cherries on paper towels to remove excess juice.

6. A sprig of holly and berries hanging from the side of a glass makes a festive drink garnish.

7. Wash your hands before cutting any drink garnishes. December *is* during the flu and cold season.

8. Use red licorice for straws. Cut a small amount off both ends to make them ready for sipping.

9. Cut tree shapes out of construction paper and punch holes in them to slide over straws. Or staple two shapes together, leaving a gap to put a straw through.

10. A combination of red and green grapes on a small skewer can add to a drink's fun. Call your grocery store to see if they carry grapes in December.

11. A fast and easy Christmas drink could be Hawaiian Punch® or green Kool-Aid®. Serve with hint #9 or #10.

12. Freeze club soda or seltzer into Christmas tree ice cube trays. Let kids place them into Hawaiian Punch® or green Kool-Aid® and watch them fizz.

13. Boil any water before freezing to make clear ice cubes or a punch bowl ring.

14. Unexpected guests can pop in delivering presents and/or singing carols, so have all the ingredients for a drink on hand to prepare something quickly. A favorite is Mexican Hot Chocolate, found on page 166.

15. Don't forget the frosty "snowballs" (miniature marshmallows) for your hot chocolate!

16. Hot drinks are an excellent choice for Christmastime, but only when you have a small group so you can keep up with the preparation and serving.

17. Punch works well at parties when guests will be coming and going at different times.

18. Make sure your punch bowl is large enough for your recipe, or only make half a recipe at a time.

19. Always have bottled or filtered water available for guests who prefer it.

20. Remember, Santa likes a big glass of milk left with his cookies!

Cold and Creamy Candy Cane Eggnog Punch

Ingredients and Supplies

Makes enough
for a party

½ gallon vanilla
ice cream

Five candy canes
(unwrapped)

Plastic bag

Rolling pin

Spoon

Tablespoon

2 quarts eggnog

One 1-liter bottle
ginger ale

Punchbowl

Miniature candy
canes (unwrapped)

Ladle

Red plastic cups

Directions

1. While the ice cream is softening, crush the five candy canes by putting them in a plastic bag and rolling them with a rolling pin.

2. Empty the ice cream into the punch bowl and stir in the candy except 1 tablespoon.

3. Put the eggnog and ginger ale into the punchbowl and stir.

4. Sprinkle the tablespoon of crushed candy canes on top of the punch mixture.

5. Hang miniature candy canes around the sides of the punchbowl.

6. Serve with the ladle into the red plastic cups, hanging a miniature candy cane on the side of each cup.

Snowball Shake

Ingredients and Supplies

Serves 6

Six 8-ounce plastic cups

Clean fresh snow (high-moisture snow is easy to pack and works best)

Knife

Two ripe bananas

Blender

4 cups vanilla ice cream

1 cup milk

Spatula

Shaved chocolate

Directions

1. Set a plastic cup down into the snow until the rim is level with the snow.

2. Pack snow around the cup as if making a snowball, careful not to get any snow inside the cup. The snow needs to be 2 to 3 inches thick around the cup.

3. Remove the "snowball cup," and flatten the bottom so it can stand on its own. Smooth out any edges and place in the freezer until you're ready to put in the shake.

4. Follow steps #1 through #3 to make five more "snowball cups." Be sure you have room in your freezer for them.

5. Slice the bananas and put them in the blender with the milk and ice cream. Blend until thick and creamy.

6. Pour the "shake" out of the blender into the snowball cups. Use your spatula to get every last yummy drop.

7. Sprinkle with the shaved chocolate.

Recyclable Santa Mug

Ingredients and Supplies

Velcro®

½-inch pink pom-pom

1-inch white pom-pom

Makes one Santa

Red baby sock

Scissors

White felt

Glue gun

Black permanent marker

Red fruit punch in barrel-shaped plastic container, 4½-inches tall

Directions

1. Stretch the baby sock (Santa's hat) around your fingers, then cut a strip of white felt to fit around the rim of the baby sock.

2. Glue the strip of white felt around the rim. It is important to glue while the sock is being stretched or it will not slide over the juice container.

3. Draw two Santa eyes on the juice container with the black permanent marker.

4. Place Santa's hat on top of the drink, with the heel of the sock standing straight up.

5. Trace the following pattern pieces onto the white felt and cut out: one beard (pattern piece #1) and one mustache (pattern piece #2).

6. Cut out five small pieces of Velcro® and attach two to the backside of the beard, two to the mustache, and one to the pink pom-pom (nose) and the other part to the juice container where the beard, mustache, and nose should go.

7. Stick the beard, mustache, and nose onto the container to finish Santa's face (as shown in illustration). The Santa pieces can be pulled off the drink and saved to make another recyclable mug.

8. Glue the white pom-pom to the toe of the baby sock.

Optional: You may also glue the beard, mustache, and pink pom-pom onto the juice container instead of using Velcro®.

Note: If you are using a different size juice container, adjust the pattern pieces accordingly, and get a larger sock if needed.

#1

#2

Crazy Rudolph Punch

Ingredients and Supplies

Make as much or as little as you like

Equal amounts of:
Cranberry juice cocktail
Storm™

Black cherry Kool-Aid® (already made)

Cherry seltzer

Punch bowl

Spoon

Ladle

Tall thin glasses

Maraschino cherries (one per drink)

Crazy straws (one per drink)

Directions

1. Pour equal amounts of the cranberry juice, Storm™, black cherry Kool-Aid®, and cherry seltzer into the punch bowl and mix.

2. Ladle the punch into tall thin glasses.

3. For each drink, push a maraschino cherry (nose) onto the end of a crazy straw, and put the straw into a glass, cherry above the punch.

Twinkling Angel Slush

Ingredients and Supplies

Makes 4 drinks

12-ounce can Hawaiian Punch

Plastic container

Hand shredder/grater

Four 8-ounce clear plastic cups

12-ounce can ginger ale

Edible glitter (found at craft stores)

Straw spoons (found at grocery stores)

Directions

1. Pour the Hawaiian Punch into a plastic container.

2. Freeze the punch overnight.

3. Using the hand shredder, grate the punch into the four plastic cups.

4. Pour 3 ounces of ginger ale on top of the punch in each cup.

5. Sprinkle edible glitter on top of the drinks.

6. Serve immediately with straw spoons.

Mexican Hot Chocolate

This is a very delicious but rich drink

Ingredients and Supplies

Makes 2 to 3 servings

Spoon or spatula

1 teaspoon cold water

1 teaspoon cornstarch

Small bowl

4 ounces Baker's® GERMAN'S® Sweet Chocolate

Medium saucepan

2 cups milk

Two to three coffee mugs

Optional: Can of whipped cream, cinnamon or cinnamon stick

Directions

1. Mix the water and cornstarch in a bowl until the mixture is dissolved. Set aside.

2. Melt the chocolate on low heat in the saucepan.

3. Add the milk and stir.

4. Turn the heat up a little and continue stirring.

5. Add the cornstarch mixture into the saucepan and continue stirring until the hot chocolate thickens. This will only take a few minutes.

6. Pour the hot chocolate into mugs.

Optional: Squirt some whipped cream on top of the hot chocolate. Sprinkle cinnamon on top or add a cinnamon stick.

Cold and Creamy Candy Cane Eggnog Punch

½ gallon vanilla ice cream
Five candy canes (unwrapped)
Plastic bag
Rolling pin
Spoon
Tablespoon
2 quarts eggnog
One 1-liter bottle ginger ale
Punchbowl
Miniature candy canes (unwrapped)
Ladle
Red plastic cups

Don't forget the camera and film

Snowball Shake

Six 8-ounce plastic cups
Clean fresh snow (high-moisture snow is easy to pack and works best)
Knife
Two ripe bananas
Blender
4 cups vanilla ice cream
1 cup milk
Spatula
Shaved chocolate

Recyclable Santa Mug

Red baby sock
Scissors
White felt
Glue gun
Black permanent marker
Red fruit punch in barrel-shaped plastic container, 4½-inches tall
Velcro®
½-inch pink pom-pom
1-inch white pom-pom

Ingredients and Supplies for Drinks

Crazy Rudolph Punch

Equal amounts of:
  Cranberry juice cocktail
  Storm™
  Black cherry Kool-Aid® (already made)
  Cherry seltzer
Punch bowl
Spoon
Ladle
Tall thin glasses
Maraschino cherries (one per drink)
Crazy straws (one per drink)

Twinkling Angel Slush

12-ounce can Hawaiian Punch
Plastic container
Hand shredder/grater
Four 8-ounce clear plastic cups
12-ounce can ginger ale

(continued)

Edible glitter (found at craft stores)
Straw spoons (found at grocery stores)

Mexican Hot Chocolate

Spoon or spatula
1 teaspoon cold water
1 teaspoon cornstarch
Small bowl
4 ounces Baker's® GERMAN'S® Sweet Chocolate
Medium saucepan
2 cups milk
Two to three coffee mugs
Optional: Can of whipped cream, cinnamon or cinnamon stick

CHAPTER 6

Christmas Potpourri

Mistletoe hanging from a doorway dates back to a Scandinavian custom when enemies who ran into each other in a forest on Christmas would suspend their fighting with a truce until the next day. Today we kiss whoever is under mistletoe, a sign of friendship.

MistleTOES

Supplies

Pencil

Green paper

Scissors

Black permanent marker

Paper fastener

Fishing line

Thumbtack

Directions

1. With the pencil, trace both feet onto the green paper, including around the toes, and cut out.

2. Use the black permanent marker to draw toenails on the toes.

3. Put the heels together and poke a paper fastener through them. Then cut, loop, and tie some fishing line on the fastener and hang the mistletoe over a doorway with a thumbtack.

Smooshies

Supplies

Heavy Christmas balloon (found at party stores)

Funnel

1 cup flour

Pencil

Directions

1. Stretch the balloon for a few minutes before filling.

2. Using the funnel, fill the balloon with 1 cup of flour. Depending on the size of the balloon you may need to add more flour. To get the flour as far down inside the balloon as possible, carefully stretch the balloon as you fill it. *Caution:* Don't poke any part of the balloon as it will cause a hole. Insert a pencil inside the opening, and stir.

3. Remove as much air as possible and tie the end of the balloon.

Note: Do not use balloons sold in packages for birthday parties. They are too thin and can break.

Hidden Christmas Words

Supplies	Paper
	Pencils

Directions

1. Hand out a piece of paper and pencil to each player. Have them spell out the word "Christmas" at the top of their paper for reference.

2. The object is for them to create as many words as possible from "Christmas." A list is below, including proper nouns.

3. They can use the letters as many times as they want. Set a 15-minute time limit.

What's the best Christmas game you've ever played? Please describe.
"Tuk, a Canadian board game my Grandfather created, involving marbles and cards. It is played in pairs and is a real cut-throat game."
—Richard L. Dmytryshyn
Littleton, Colorado

Christmas

Hat	Match	Catch	Ash
Is	Arm	Maria	Crash
Sit	Rich	Smart	Hash
It	Cast	Tar	Mama
Chris	Scratch	Christ	That
Cat	Star	Tim	Sarah
Hit	March	Miss	Ham
Rat	Start	Matt	Sam
Car	Art	Sir	Mist
Hair	Act	Scar	Mars
Air	This	Smash	Am
Chair	Cart	Trash	Tara
Mat	His	Starch	Ha Ha
At	As	Access	Sahara
Sat	Mass	Arch	Mast
A	Hatch	Carat	Thatch

171

Christmas Word Search

1. Advent
2. Angel
3. Bethlehem
4. Candle
5. Candy Cane
6. Carolers
7. Christmas Tree
8. Cookies
9. Deck the Halls
10. Decoration
11. Egg Nog
12. Elf
13. Epiphany
14. First Noel
15. Frosty the Snowman
16. Fun
17. Gingerbread House
18. Ho Ho Ho
19. Jingle Bells
20. Joy to the World
21. Lights
22. Merry Christmas
23. Mittens
24. Mistletoe
25. Mrs. Santa Claus
26. Nativity
27. Naughty
28. New Year's
29. North Pole
30. Nutcracker
31. Ornaments
32. Poinsettia
33. Presents
34. Reindeer
35. Rudolph
36. Santa Claus
37. Santa's List
38. Scrooge
39. Sleigh
40. Silent Night
41. Snow
42. Snowflake
43. Star
44. Stocking
45. Tradition
46. Train
47. Three Wise Men
48. Toy
49. Tree Stand
50. Wreath

Supplies

Copies of the word search (one per person)
Pencils

Directions

1. There are 50 hidden words and phrases. Search for them. They might be spelled forward, backward, diagonally, up, or down.

2. Circle as many as possible. Good Luck!

```
M R S S A N T A C L A U S T F E
E L O P H T R O N S Z N Y U R P
R L Z E N A C Y D N A C N R O I
R P F D E C K T H E H A L L S P
Y T T F A C S R A E Y W E N T H
C H R I S T M A S T R E E P Y A
H R E R X S N O I T I D A R T N
R E E S Z I S S T E A Y Q S H Y
I E S T Y L E R R O A Q R I E S
S W T N E S I E P H S X A L S T
T I A O K A K E A O N M T E N N
M S N E A T O D P H E Z S N O E
A E D L L N O N A O Y A Z T W S
S M S I F A C I T H Z B N N M E
E E N G W S L E I G H A A I A R
S N E H O C L R O L U I T G N P
U O T T N T S R E G F T I H S Q
O I T S S A D G H T I T V T D D
H T I I L K N T P R J E I Q L O
D A M E H A Y A E B G S T J R S
A R E L T Q R K I G C N Y U O O
E O H D A T C D N R W I D P W T
R C E N E A E O O R T O Q T E G
B E L A R A G O A A L P N Z H N
R D H C W Q G P S P Q X Y S T I
E A T R R E W Y H S T R P W O K
G U E T A D V E N T N I A R T C
N B B P Z T C A R O L E R S Y O
I C D S O X S T N E M A N R O T
G I A Y S L L E B E L G N I J S
```

Supplies for Christmas Potpourri

MistleTOES

Pencil
Green paper
Scissors
Black permanent
 marker
Paper fastener
Fishing line
Thumbtack

Smooshies

Heavy Christmas balloon
 (found at party stores)
Funnel
1 cup flour
Pencil

Hidden Christmas Words

Paper
Pencils

Christmas Word Search

Copies of the word
 search (one per
 person)
Pencils

Don't forget the camera and film

173

CHAPTER 7
New Year's Tips, and Fun Party Ideas

Midnight

Supplies	
No more than 13 can play this game at any time	Paper
	Pen
Deck of cards	Serpentine throws (found at party stores)

Dick Clark just signed another contract and will be "dropping the ball" in New York City's Times Square at least until the year 2005.

What does it mean to make a New Year's resolution? "Make a promise to change something and keep that promise, like get better grades in school."
—Sean Ayers, Age 13 Toledo, Ohio

Directions

1. Separate the cards into "four of a kind," for example, four aces, four eights, and so on. They do not have to be in order.

2. You will need one set of four per player. Put the cards you don't need away.

3. Write everyone's name on the paper in a column on the left. Ask someone to record "scores" in the right column.

4. Separate the serpentines. You will need one less serpentine throw than the number of players. Have the players sit in a circle around a table or on the floor and put the serpentine throws in the middle.

5. Shuffle the cards and deal one at a time to the players, going clockwise, until the cards are all distributed. Each player should have four cards.

6. On the word "Go," have the players quickly pass any one card from their hands of four to the player to their left while collecting one from the player to their right.

7. They keep passing cards quickly until one player gets "four of a kind." That person quietly takes a serpentine throw from the middle. Each player who notices also grabs a serpentine, until all are gone.

8. The player without a serpentine gets the letter "M" from the word "MIDNIGHT," written on the paper next to his name.

9. Play another round, with the serpentine throws back in the middle. If the same player doesn't get a serpentine, he gets the next letter "I." If a new player is left without a serpentine, he gets the letter "M."

10. Play until someone has "MIDNIGHT" next to his name.

New Year's Karaoke

Supplies

Karaoke machine with *Auld Lang Syne*
Prize for winner

Directions

1. Without using the Karaoke machine screen to display the words, play the music to *Auld Lang Syne* and take turns singing the words.

2. Award the prize to the person who comes the closest to singing the whole song correctly.

3. Then take turns, or all sing *Auld Lang Syne* together, with the help of the Karaoke machine screen.

How did you celebrate the Millennium New Year's?
"Dancing all night long—what better way to not worry if the world would come to an end."
—Mimi Thiele
San Diego, California

Should auld acquaintance be forgot....

White Elephant Gift Exchange

Supplies

Wrapped gifts brought by guests

Extra wrapped gifts for guests who forget

Scissors

Paper

Pen

Bowl

What is a good Christmas gift? What was the best gift you ever gave? "One given from the heart, a video tour of my house when my husband and I were first married. I sent it to my aunt in Florida because she was too ill to come back to Pennsylvania. When she died three years later, my uncle told me she'd play that tape over and over and over. He said it was one of the best things she ever received."

—Pamela Kennedy
Plum, Pennsylvania

Directions

1. Ask everyone to bring a wrapped gift for a White Elephant Gift Exchange—an item they don't want. It could be anything, a present they got for Christmas or something from around the house.

2. Cut a small piece of paper per guest, and number them starting at "1." Fold and put them in a bowl, and have each guest draw out one piece.

3. Place all the gifts in the middle of the floor or table with your guests in a circle around them.

4. The player with "1" goes first. He chooses a present from the pile, opens it, and places it in front of him.

5. Then the player with "2" decides if he would like to "steal" the first player's gift or choose a gift from the pile. If he steals the first player's gift, that player chooses another gift from the pile.

6. The game continues, with each player choosing a gift from the pile or stealing from another player, until the last player has taken his turn. Then the first player takes the last turn, stealing from someone or opting to keep his gift.

7. Three times works best for the amount of times one gift can be stolen. Set this rule before beginning the game. Remember to tell your guests they can bring their gifts back next year if they don't like them!

Note: It's best to play this game with either adults or children, not both. Or have each age group play its own game.

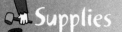

Happy New Year's Hat

Supplies

Scissors

Card stock

Markers

Paper hole puncher

3 inches gold cording

Hat with removable glitter band that says "Happy New Year"

Stapler

Tissue paper

Shredded color paper

Vitamin C roll

Individual champagne bottle (also available in non-alcoholic)

Gold-wrapped chocolate coins in mesh bag

Wrapped fortune cookie

8½ x 11-inch piece New Year's paper

Optional: Computer

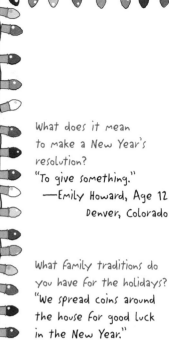

Directions

1. To make a wisdom booklet , first cut the card stock into 1 x 3-inch strips.

2. With the markers, write inspirational sayings of your own or ones from a book onto the card stock strips.

3. Punch a hole in the left top corner of each strip. Thread the gold cording through all the holes, then tie to hold the wisdom booklet together.

4. Pull the removable glitter band off the hat. Turn the hat on its top and staple the glitter band back on the hat, in the same place, but with the "Happy New Year" right side up.

5. Crumple tissue paper in the hat then put shredded paper on top.

6. Lay the roll of vitamin C, champagne bottle, chocolate coins, wisdom booklet, and fortune cookie in the hat.

7. Write the following explanation on the New Year's paper, and include it in the hat:

   Our New Year's Gift to You:
   Health - Vitamin C
   Happiness - Champagne
   Wealth - Chocolate Coins
   Wisdom - Wisdom Booklet
   Good Fortune - Fortune Cookie

   Directions:
   Chew Vitamin C while drinking Champagne. Soon you will feel great. Then eat Chocolate Coins while reading our Wisdom Booklet. Now you are smart. Open the Fortune Cookie and hope for the best. Have a Great New Year!

Optional: Type the wisdom booklet and explanation on the computer.

Crafts and Favors

New Year's Ball Drop

How are the holidays different in your country? "New Year's is the biggest family event in Japan. Therefore we make a special dish called osechi and enjoy it with the family. My father often works, even on New Year's Day, so we wait to have our New Year's dish till he comes home. At the table, my father addresses each family member. All family members tell their New Year's resolutions."

—Masako Matumoto Mizuho, Nagoya Japan

Supplies

Beach ball (works the best)

Silver or gold glitter spray paint

Paintbrush

Red acrylic paint

10 feet household twine

1-inch screw eye

Scissors

Poster board

Markers

Directions

1. Blow up the beach ball. Spray paint the ball silver or gold and let it dry.

2. Paint the year on the ball with the black paint and let dry.

3. Tie the twine to the beach ball's nozzle.

4. Thread the opposite end of twine through the screw eye.

5. Fit the screw eye into a small nail hole in the wall or ceiling.

6. Cut the poster board in half, lengthwise.

7. Tape half the poster board vertically next to the "ball drop." With the markers, write large hours, starting with "6 pm," on the bottom and work your way up to "12 midnight."

8. Position the ball by the hour on the poster board you'd like to start, and secure the twine by laying it on the floor with a weight on it, or by tying it off to a chair, table, or a nail in the wall.

9. Every hour, unleash the twine, pull it down to raise your ball to the next hour, and secure it until the next hour.

10. Ten seconds before midnight, unleash the twine and count aloud from ten to zero, letting the twine slide between your fingers to drop the ball.

Note: If you can't find a beach ball, use a light 10 x 12-inch ball, only tape the twine to it.

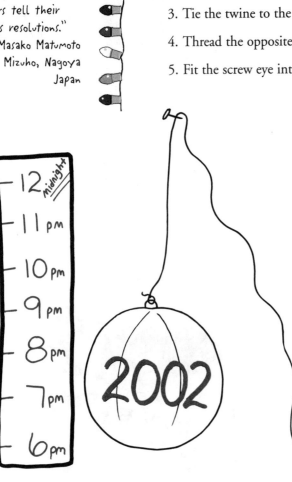

Personalized Champagne Bottle

Supplies

Bottle of champagne (also available in non-alcoholic)

Computer

3⅓ x 4-inch shipping label (found at office stores)

Optional: Markers

Directions

1. Soak the label off the champagne bottle and dry the bottle.

2. Type your own personalized message on the computer, including the year. Use designs to make it as elaborate as you like.

3. Print your message on the label, then peel and stick the label onto the bottle.

Optional: Use markers to design a label for the bottle.

For many, the start of the New Year starts on a different day and even in a different month than the first of January. The Chinese New Year falls in February. The Jewish New Year, Rosh Hashanah, is celebrated in September.

How did you celebrate the Millennium New Year's?
"All day, starting with the first country and going until Hawaii! Every hour we would shout 'Happy New Year' and kiss each other."

—Shalaine Root
Thornton, Colorado

Nutty Popcorn

Ingredients and Supplies

Serves 4

½ cup butter

Saucepan

7 to 8 cups popped popcorn

Cookie sheet

½ cup brown sugar

½ cup corn syrup

½ teaspoon salt

Spoon or spatula

1 cup mixed nuts

Wax paper

Directions

1. Melt the butter in the saucepan.

2. Lay the popcorn on the cookie sheet.

3. Add the brown sugar, corn syrup, and salt to the melted butter. Mix well and bring to a boil while stirring constantly.

4. Pour the mixture over the popcorn, add the nuts, and quickly stir all together.

5. Bake for 15 minutes at 350°.

6. Dump the "nutty popcorn" onto wax paper and cool for 30 to 45 minutes.

7. Store uncovered.

What is the best Christmas gift you received as an adult? "A cookbook of my favorite Ukrainian recipes, ones that my eighty-year-old Grandma had created from scratch and then wrote longhand." —Richard L. Dmytryshyn Littleton, Colorado

New Year's Number Cake

Ingredients and Supplies

Makes enough for a party

Two cake mixes

Two 13 x 9-inch cake pans

Knife

Aluminum foil

Large cookie sheet

Two 16-ounce cans frosting, any flavor

Directions

1. Make the cakes according to the package directions, pouring one cake into each pan. Cool.

2. Cut each cake in half, then each half into a number to spell out the year.

3. Lay the "number cake" out on a foil-covered cookie sheet and frost.

What family traditions do you have for the holidays, including New Year's? "Our family tradition is sauerkraut and pork at midnight on New Year's, a German tradition to bring good luck." —Danielle Dell San Diego, California

Holiday Goodies

2002

New Year's Eve Taco Dip

Ingredients and Supplies

Serves 12

16 ounces cream cheese

16 ounces sour cream

Mixer and bowl

Spatula or spoon

Two 10 or 12-inch platters

16 ounces salsa

Four thinly sliced green onions

¾ cup diced green pepper

1 cup diced tomatoes

6 ounces sliced black olives

2½ cups shredded cheddar cheese

Directions

1. Let the cream cheese soften on the counter, in the wrapper, about 2 hours.

2. Mix the cream cheese and sour cream together in the bowl until creamy.

3. Divide and spread the mixture onto the platters.

4. Pour the salsa over the mixture and spread it out.

5. Sprinkle the green onions, green pepper, and tomatoes on top of the salsa, in that order.

6. Sprinkle the olives over that, and then top with the cheese.

7. Refrigerate for an hour or more if you can wait.

8. Serve with tortilla chips.

Note: This dip is so good, it goes fast. That's why the recipe is for two plates. Make one for a party and save one for yourself. It makes an excellent dinner.

How do you celebrate New Year's?

"I celebrate Chinese New Year's in February. Adults give out money to the children, because they believe it will give them good luck. If they don't, they will have bad luck. The younger the children, the more money they will get. We also give offerings to the people in our family who have passed away."
—Sonya Vo, Age 11
Littleton, Colorado

Kids' Iced Apple Juice

Ingredients and Supplies

Serves 4   Ice bucket

4 cups rock candy

Four individual bottles apple juice

Directions

1. Chill the apple juice until you are ready to serve.

2. Fill the bucket with the bottles of apple juice.

3. Surround the bottles with rock candy to represent ice.

4. Have each child take an apple juice and a handful of candy.

Pineapple Champagne New Year's Punch

Ingredients and Supplies

Serves about 2 dozen people

3 cups pineapple juice

¼ cup lemon juice

64-ounce bottle guava juice

Bottle of champagne

Quart of pineapple sherbet

Punch bowl and ladle

Spoon

2 dozen New Year's cups

Directions

1. Chill all the ingredients overnight. Keep the sherbet frozen.

2. Pour all the ingredients into the punch bowl, except the sherbet. Stir.

3. Put the sherbet into the punch right before serving, and mix.

4. When the sherbet has slightly melted, ladle into the cups to toast in the New Year.

Drinks

Ingredients and Supplies for New Year's Tips, and Fun Party Ideas

Midnight

Deck of cards
Paper
Pen
Serpentine throws
  (found at party stores)

New Year's Karaoke

Karaoke machine
  with Auld Lang Syne
Prize for winner

White Elephant Gift Exchange

Wrapped gifts brought
  by guests
Extra wrapped gifts for
  guests who forget
Scissors
Paper
Pen
Bowl

Happy New Year's Hat

Scissors
Card stock
Markers
Paper hole puncher
3 inches gold cording
Hat with removable
  glitter band that says
  "Happy New Year"
Stapler
Tissue paper
Shredded color paper
Vitamin C roll

(continued)

Individual champagne
  bottle (also available in
  non-alcoholic)
Gold-wrapped chocolate
  coins in mesh bag
Wrapped fortune cookie
8½ x 11-inch piece New
  Year's paper
Optional: Computer

New Year's Ball Drop

Beach ball (works the best)
Silver or gold glitter
  spray paint
Paintbrush
Black acrylic paint
10 feet household twine
1-inch screw eye
Scissors
Poster board
Markers

Personalized Champagne Bottle

Bottle of champagne
  (also available in non-
  alcoholic)
Computer
3⅓ x 4-inch shipping
  label (found at office
  stores)
Optional: Markers

Nutty Popcorn

½ cup butter
Saucepan
7 to 8 cups popped
  popcorn
Cookie sheet
½ cup brown sugar
½ cup corn syrup
½ teaspoon salt
Spoon or spatula
1 cup mixed nuts
Wax paper

New Year's Number Cake

Two cake mixes
Two 13 x 9-inch cake pans
Knife
Aluminum foil
Large cookie sheet
Two 16-ounce cans
  frosting, any flavor

New Year's Eve Taco Dip

16 ounces cream cheese
16 ounces sour cream
Mixer and bowl
Spatula or spoon
Two 10 or 12-inch platters
16 ounces salsa
Four thinly sliced
  green onions

(continued)

¾ cup diced green pepper
1 cup diced tomatoes
6 ounces sliced black
  olives
2½ cups shredded
  cheddar cheese

Kids' Iced Apple Juice

Ice bucket
4 cups rock candy
Four individual bottles
  apple juice

Pineapple Champagne New Year's Punch

3 cups pineapple juice
¼ cup lemon juice
64-ounce bottle
  guava juice
Bottle of champagne
Quart of pineapple sherbet
Punch bowl and ladle
Spoon
2 dozen New Year's cups

New Year's Traditions and Superstitions from Around the World

Philippines

To be sure that the upcoming year is going to be bright, turn all your lights on at midnight.

An animal noise heard at midnight determines things about the upcoming year, such as a cow eating grass means your year will be abundant.

If it's sunny on January 1, the rest of the year will also be sunny. If it's an icky day, you will have an icky year.

If you leave your home on New Year's Day, you will be away from your family a lot.

Ireland

Girls place leaves under their pillows on New Year's Eve to have dreams about who they are going to marry.

To be sure to have plenty of food in the New Year, eat everything in your house before January 1.

Brazil

When midnight strikes, each woman has to meet three men before she meets another woman. The same goes for men. This means they will have luck when it comes to love.

More

All ages love stomping on bubble wrap. It's sure to bring an extra "POP" to your party.

Set lots of alarm clocks to go off at midnight.

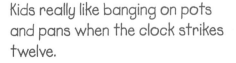

Kids really like banging on pots and pans when the clock strikes twelve.

Midnight Fun

Put fun in the air by blowing bubbles, watching as they "BURST"!

Time to dream... what does the New Year hold for you?

Time to celebrate! Be the best dressed at the party.

Make a New Year's resolution tablecloth. Everyone uses a permanent marker to write a resolution on a tablecloth. Use your tablecloth every year—you'll have fun reading the old resolutions and adding new ones.

New Year's Traditions and Superstitions from Around the World (continued)

Italy
If you give a present of honey, it's a wish for peace for you and the recipient.

Iran
You will receive good fortune by displaying a New Year's table.

India
Immediately in the morning, you should look at something beautiful and excellent.

Vietnam
The first person to come into your home at the beginning of the New Year will have an influence in your life for the next year.

Put a rope in front of your home to keep out evil spirits.

Join hands and sing Auld Lang Syne at midnight to recall the past and have a good New Year.

Final Thoughts

Dashing through the snow.
To write another book I go....

Till next time
Willie.

Index

Order Form

Become an expert the easy way! Order from the **What Do I Do?**® series

CALL OUR TOLL FREE HOTLINE TO ORDER TODAY AT:

1-888-738-1733

Oakbrook Publishing House

P.O. Box 2463 • Littleton, CO 80161-2463

PHONE: (303) 738-1733 • **FAX:** (303) 797-1995

WEBSITE: http://www.whatdoidobooks.com

E-MAIL: Oakbrook@whatdoidobooks.com

NAME: _____

ADDRESS: _____

CITY, STATE & ZIP CODE: _____ **PHONE:** (___) _____

Order 2 books and get a 10% discount, or order 3 or more books and get a 10% discount and free shipping.

BOOK TITLE	QUANTITY	PRICE	TOTAL
Christmas Parties...What Do I Do?® ISBN: 0-9649939-4-5	_____	$19.95 ea.	$ _____
Halloween School Parties ...What Do I Do?® ISBN: 0-9649939-8-8	_____	$19.95 ea.	$ _____
NEW *Slumber Parties...What Do I Do?*® ISBN: 0-9649939-0-2 *(available after May 2001)*	_____	$19.95 ea.	$ _____
Valentine Boxes...What Do I Do?® ISBN: 0-9649939-3-7	_____	$12.95 ea.	$ _____
Valentine School Parties...What Do I Do?® ISBN: 0-9649939-9-6	_____	$19.95 ea.	$ _____

SUBTOTAL	$_____
DISCOUNT	$_____
SUBTOTAL	$_____
Colorado Res. Add 3.8% Sales Tax	$_____
Shipping & Handling (see below)	$_____
TOTAL	$_____

100% fully guaranteed on all orders

CHECK OR MONEY ORDER PAYABLE TO: Oakbrook Publishing House

CREDIT CARD: ☐ Visa ☐ Master Card ☐ Discover

CARD NUMBER _____ **EXP. DATE** _____

SIGNATURE _____

Canadian orders must be accompanied by a postal money order in U.S. funds.

SHIPPING AND HANDLING CHARGES ARE:
1st class $3.75, 4th class $2.25 (Allow 7-10 days for 4th class mail), additional books add $1.15 each.

SCHOOL SPECIAL
Purchase 5 books from the **What Do I Do**® series and get 1 book free.
Purchase 10 books and get 2 free and free shipping.
Get an order together, ask other parents, teachers, or friends and get free books to be used in the school library or PTO room.

Order Form

Become an expert the easy way! Order from the **What Do I Do?**® series

CALL OUR TOLL FREE HOTLINE TO ORDER TODAY AT:

1-888-738-1733

Oakbrook Publishing House

P.O. Box 2463 • Littleton, CO 80161-2463

PHONE: (303) 738-1733 • **FAX:** (303) 797-1995

WEBSITE: http://www.whatdoidobooks.com

E-MAIL: Oakbrook@whatdoidobooks.com

NAME: _____

ADDRESS: _____

CITY, STATE & ZIP CODE: _____ **PHONE: (** **)** _____

Order 2 books and get a 10% discount, or order 3 or more books and get a 10% discount and free shipping.

BOOK TITLE	QUANTITY	PRICE	TOTAL
Christmas Parties...What Do I Do?® ISBN: 0-9649939-4-5	_____	$19.95 ea.	$ _____
Halloween School Parties ...What Do I Do?® ISBN: 0-9649939-8-8	_____	$19.95 ea.	$ _____
NEW **Slumber Parties...What Do I Do?**® ISBN: 0-9649939-0-2 *(available after May 2001)*	_____	$19.95 ea.	$ _____
Valentine Boxes...What Do I Do?® ISBN: 0-9649939-3-7	_____	$12.95 ea.	$ _____
Valentine School Parties...What Do I Do?® ISBN: 0-9649939-9-6	_____	$19.95 ea.	$ _____

SUBTOTAL	$_____
DISCOUNT	$_____
SUBTOTAL	$_____
Colorado Res. Add 3.8% Sales Tax	$_____
Shipping & Handling (see below)	$_____
TOTAL	$_____

100% fully guaranteed on all orders

CHECK OR MONEY ORDER PAYABLE TO: Oakbrook Publishing House

CREDIT CARD: ☐ Visa   ☐ Master Card   ☐ Discover

CARD NUMBER _____ **EXP. DATE** _____

SIGNATURE _____

Canadian orders must be accompanied by a postal money order in U.S. funds.

SHIPPING AND HANDLING CHARGES ARE:
1st class $3.75, 4th class $2.25 (Allow 7-10 days for 4th class mail), additional books add $1.15 each.

SCHOOL SPECIAL
Purchase 5 books from the **What Do I Do**® series and get 1 book free.
Purchase 10 books and get 2 free and free shipping.
Get an order together, ask other parents, teachers, or friends and get free books to be used in the school library or PTO room.